Vector-borne Diseases on Fire Island, New York
(Fire Island National Seashore Science Synthesis Paper)

Technical Report NPS/NER/NRTR--2005/018

Howard S. Ginsberg

USGS Patuxent Wildlife Research Center
Coastal Field Station, Woodward Hall-PLS
University of Rhode Island
Kingston, RI 02881

September 2005

U.S. Department of the Interior
National Park Service
Northeast Region
Boston, Massachusetts

The Northeast Region of the National Park Service (NPS) comprises national parks and related areas in 13 New England and Mid-Atlantic states. The diversity of parks and their resources are reflected in their designations as national parks, seashores, historic sites, recreation areas, military parks, memorials, and rivers and trails. Biological, physical, and social science research results, natural resource inventory and monitoring data, scientific literature reviews, bibliographies, and proceedings of technical workshops and conferences related to these park units are disseminated through the NPS/NER Technical Report (NRTR) and Natural Resources Report (NRR) series. The reports are a continuation of series with previous acronyms of NPS/PHSO, NPS/MAR, NPS/BSO-RNR and NPS/NERBOST. Individual parks may also disseminate information through their own report series.

Natural Resources Reports are the designated medium for information on technologies and resource management methods; "how to" resource management papers; proceedings of resource management workshops or conferences; and natural resource program descriptions and resource action plans.

Technical Reports are the designated medium for initially disseminating data and results of biological, physical, and social science research that addresses natural resource management issues; natural resource inventories and monitoring activities; scientific literature reviews; bibliographies; and peer-reviewed proceedings of technical workshops, conferences, or symposia.

Mention of trade names or commercial products does not constitute endorsement or recommendation for use by the National Park Service.

The statements, findings, conclusions, recommendations, and data in this report are solely those of the author(s), and do not necessarily reflect the views of the U.S. Department of the Interior, National Park Service.

Print copies of reports in these series, produced in limited quantity and only available as long as the supply lasts, or preferably, file copies on CD, may be obtained by sending a request to the address on the back cover. Print copies also may be requested from the NPS Technical Information Center (TIC), Denver Service Center, PO Box 25287, Denver, CO 80225-0287. A copy charge may be involved. To order from TIC, refer to document D-110.

This report may also be available as a downloadable portable document format file from the Internet at http://www.nps.gov/nero/science/.

Please cite this publication as:

Ginsberg, H.S. September 2005. Vector-borne diseases of Fire Island, New York (Fire Island National Seashore Science Synthesis Paper). Technical Report NPS/NER/NRTR--2005/018. National Park Service. Boston, MA.

PREFACE

FIRE ISLAND NATIONAL SEASHORE
Science Synthesis Papers to Support Preparation of a
General Management Plan

BACKGROUND AND PURPOSE

Fire Island National Seashore (FIIS) is scheduled to begin preparation of a new General Management Plan (GMP) in the near future. A GMP outlines how natural and cultural resources, public uses, and park operations should be managed over the next several decades. The GMP addresses significant issues or challenges that are facing the park, proposes management solutions, and establishes management priorities. The Fire Island GMP will be prepared by a team of planners, with input from the park, technical subject matter experts, and with substantial public involvement.

To insure that the GMP team has all relevant natural resource information available to them, a series of scientific synthesis papers has been prepared for a variety of natural resource topics that will be of special relevance to the Fire Island GMP. Based on a 2-day meeting with the FIIS Superintendent, FIIS Chief of Natural Resource Management, Northeast Region planners, and Northeast Region science staff, the following natural resource topic areas were identified;

- Geomorphology of beaches and dunes
- Physical processes of the bay shoreline
- Habitat ecology and water quality of Great South Bay
- Conservation of Living Marine Resources (habitats, finfish and shellfish)
- Vector-borne diseases
- White-tailed Deer ecology and management

For each of these topics, leading scientific experts were invited to prepare papers that synthesize our current state-of-knowledge. There is a wealth of published technical information on these topics. The purpose of these papers was to provide a scientifically credible summary of the available and relevant information and present this information in a succinct manner. The GMP team will receive papers that provide an objective, independent and expert synthesis of an extensive and often complex technical literature. Each paper was subject to the scientific peer review process.

Each synthesis paper is expected to accomplish the following;

- Synthesize and interpret the relevant literature and monitoring data to describe the fundamental processes controlling the natural resource, and describe historic and recent trends or rates of change for relevant processes, habitats, or species.
- Describe current and historic management, regulatory, and other activities that have been relevant to the particular natural resource.
- Identify gaps in our current understanding of the natural resource.

Because the synthesis papers are prepared prior to initiation of the GMP process, if information gaps are considered critical to decision-making for the GMP there may be adequate time to conduct the appropriate required studies or data analysis tasks. Moreover, the papers will serve to identify topics or issues that should be the focus of additional synthesis or review papers in support of the GMP information gathering and synthesis phase.

OVERVIEW OF THE PAPERS

These summaries are derived, with some editing, directly from the individual papers.

The Coastal Geomorphology of Fire Island: a Portrait of Continuity and Change
Technical Report NPS/NER/NRTR--2005/021

Authors: Norbert P. Psuty, Michele Grace, and Jeffrey P. Pace
             Rutgers University

Summary: Fire Island has a well-developed beach on the ocean side and is dominated by a variety of dune features, reaching elevations of 11-13m. Much of the island is undeveloped and retains a wide array of coastal dune forms in near natural condition. However, there are a number of residential communities, primarily on the western portion of Fire Island, that have altered the landscape and geomorphological processes. The controlled inlets at either end of the island are a type of interactive feature that have particular roles in the passage of sand along the shore. Thus, the geomorphological characteristics and configuration of the island are products of a suite of natural processes, complemented by human actions. This paper describes the landforms (beaches, dunes, inlets, and barrier island gaps) and basic controls on these landforms, such as tides, wave climate, storm history, the availability and rate of supply of sediment, and sea level rise.

There is insufficient sediment coming to Fire Island from all of the potential sources to maintain the entire system. There is evidence of erosion on all parts of the island, except the artificially-created Democrat Point. The sediment deficits are greatest along the eastern portion of the island, but are buffered in the central and western area because of the contributions from an offshore source. The recent acceleration in sea-level rise, coupled with the general negative sediment budget, will result in continued beach erosion and dune displacement, with greater effects occurring in the eastern portion of the island.

During the peer review process, it was determined that a follow-up synthesis paper should be prepared that specifically focuses on the response of Fire Island beaches and dunes to human activities, including ORV traffic, structures, sand fencing, beach scraping, and other activities. This paper is presently being developed.

Bay Shoreline Physical Processes, Fire Island
Technical Report NPS/NER/NRTR--2005/020

Authors: Karl F. Nordstrom, Rutgers University
             Nancy L. Jackson, New Jersey Institute of Technology

Summary: Wave and current energies on the bay side of Fire Island are low, but much of the bay shoreline is eroding. The greatest changes occur near inlets or next to marinas and bulkheads. Inlets, overwash and dune migration deliver sediment from the ocean to the bay where it forms substrate that evolves into tidal flats, marshes and beaches. These sediment inputs allow barrier islands to maintain themselves as they migrate landward under the influence of sea level rise. The creation and migration of inlets in the past extended their influence well beyond locations of present inlets.

About 17.0 km of the 49.5 km long bay shoreline of Fire Island is marsh; 24.5 km is beach; and 8.0 km is fronted by bulkheads, marina breakwaters and docks. The biggest constraints to allowing Fire Island to undergo natural dynamism are the desire to protect private properties on the island from erosion and overwash and the need to protect the mainland from flooding due to formation of new inlets. Bulkheads are common on the bay shore in developed communities. These structures replace natural formations landward of them and prevent sand from entering the littoral drift system, causing sediment starvation in unprotected areas downdrift. These adverse effects can be reduced by replacing lost sediment by beach nourishment. Use of beach fill on the low tide terrace covers benthic habitat. This problem could be avoided by placing fill above the mean high water mark, creating an eroding feeder upland.

Dune building projects on the oceanside and construction of bulkheads on the bayside restrict the delivery of sediment by inlets, wave overwash and aeolian transport. Temporary inlets would provide some sediment, but artificial closure by human efforts would limit these inputs to a much smaller area than in the past.

Future sea levels are expected to rise at a greater rate, causing increased frequency of overwash and creation of new inlets if not prevented by beach nourishment and dune-building projects on the oceanside. Elimination of the delivery of sediment to the bayside by these natural processes will result in continued retreat of the bay shoreline into the higher portions of the barrier island, resulting in loss of marsh habitat, increase in open water habitat, and truncation of cross-shore environmental gradients.

Water Quality and Ecology of Great South Bay
Technical Report NPS/NER/NRTR--2005/019
Author: Kenneth R. Hinga
                 University of Rhode Island

Summary: The overall objective of this paper is to present a short synopsis of information on the characteristics of water quality and ecology of the Great South Bay, with particular attention to the waters within the boundaries of Fire Island National Seashore (FIIS), where possible. This report serves as an update and addition to the report *Estuarine Resources of the Fire Island National Seashore and Vicinity* (Bokuniewicz et al., 1993). Great South Bay is approximately 45 km long, with a maximum width of about 11 km. The Bay is shallow, with an average depth at mean low water of just 1.3m.

Regarding water quality, a review of bacterial indicator monitoring data suggests that some bayside beaches and marinas of Fire Island have had fecal coliform concentrations that are at or approaching levels of concern, but in general the levels are quite acceptable. Nutrient enrichment is an issue for all shallow, enclosed, lagoon-type estuaries, like Great South Bay. There is an encouraging trend of decreasing dissolved inorganic nitrogen in Great South Bay over the past quarter century. Coincident with the decline in nitrogen, there appears to be a trend of decreasing primary production, as determined by measuring phytoplankton chlorophyll concentration, over the past 15 years. Historically, portions of Great South Bay (e.g., near and in Moriches Bay) experienced intense phytoplankton blooms, probably attributed to discharges from duck farms. Since 1985, a brown tide has occurred periodically to disruptive levels in the Bay. Brown tide blooms can cause significant mortalities of hard clams and can damage seagrass beds because the blooms prevent light sufficient to support growth of the seagrass species. The densest seagrass beds in the Bay are found along the shallow shoreline of the Seashore.

Conservation and Management of Living Marine Resources
Technical Report NPS/NER/NRTR--2005/023
Authors: David O. Conover, Robert Cerrato, and William Wise
            Stony Brook University

Summary: The finfish species likely to be landed by commercial harvesters from Fire Island NS or nearby waters are bluefish, winter flounder, summer flounder, weakfish, Atlantic silversides, and menhaden. The recreational species landed within the Bay have not been described in detail since the 1960s, but total recreational landings for New York as a whole suggest that fluke, winter flounder, bluefish, weakfish, tautog, and black sea bass are the main species. Some of the fish species landed in the Seashore region are present only transiently as older juveniles and adults. Such species would include striped bass, menhaden, eels, and weakfish. These species do not use the Bay as a spawning and nursery area. Other species use Fire Island waters as both nursery grounds for young-of-the-year (YOY) stages as well as adults. The value of Seashore estuarine habitats for these species is great (bluefish, winter flounder, fluke, tautog, black sea bass). Ecologically important species, those that are an important forage species for piscivorous fishes, include Atlantic silversides, bay anchovy, sand lance, northern pipefish, and others. Killifishes are a major component of the fish fauna of salt marsh habitats. Shellfish of potential recreational or commercial value found within Seashore boundaries include surfclam, hard clam, blue mussel, soft clam, oyster, bay scallop, razor clam, conch, blue crab, Jonah crab, rock crab, lady crab, spider crab, and horseshoe crab (although not technically classified as shellfish). Generally, there has been a dramatic decline in the commercial harvest of shellfish species from the Bay. For example, since 1976 the harvest of hard clams has declined 100 fold. It is recommended that the Seashore take a leadership role in reaching out cooperatively to government and non-government agencies toward encouraging restoration of Great South Bay living marine resources and increasing public awareness of coastal zone management issues.

Vector-borne Diseases on Fire Island
Technical Report NPS/NER/NRTR--2005/018
Author: Howard S. Ginsberg
            USGS-Patuxent Wildlife Research Center

Summary: This paper discusses eleven tick-borne and five mosquito-borne pathogens that are known to occur at FIIS, or could potentially occur. The potential for future occurrence, and ecological factors that influence occurrence, are assessed for each disease. Lyme disease is the most common vector-borne disease on Fire Island. The Lyme spirochete, *Borrelia burgdorferi*, is endemic in local tick and wildlife populations. Public education, personal precautions against tick bite, and prompt treatment of early-stage infections can help manage the risk of Lyme disease on Fire Island. The pathogens that cause Human Monocytic Ehrlichiosis and Tularemia have been isolated from ticks or wildlife on Fire Island, and conditions suggest that other tick-borne diseases (including Babesiosis, Rocky Mountain Spotted Fever, and Human Granulocytic Ehrlichiosis) might also occur, but these are far less common than Lyme disease, if present.

West Nile Virus (WNV) is the primary mosquito-borne human pathogen that is known to occur on Fire Island. Ecological conditions and recent epizootiological events suggest that WNV occurs in foci that can shift from year to year. Therefore, a surveillance program with appropriate responses to increasing epizootic activity can help manage the risk of WNV transmission on Fire Island.

White-tailed Deer Ecology and Management on Fire Island
Technical Report NPS/NER/NRTR--2005/022

Author: H. Brian Underwood
                USGS-Patuxent Wildlife Research Center

Summary: Deer populations have grown dramatically on Fire Island National Seashore (FIIS) since 1983. Trend data reveal a dichotomy in deer dynamics. In the eastern half of the island, deer density appears to have stabilized between 25-35 deer/km^2. In the western half of the island, deer densities are 3-4 times as high in residential communities. Concomitant with that increase has been a general decline in physical stature of some animals, visible impacts on island vegetation, especially in the Sunken Forest, and a perceived increase in the frequency of human and deer interactions. Intensive research on FIIS has shown that deer occupy relatively predictable home ranges throughout the year, but can and do move up and down the island. Impacts of deer on vegetation are most dramatic in the Sunken Forest. Most obvious are the effects of browsing on the herb layer of the Sunken Forest. The least obvious, but perhaps more significant impact is the stark lack of regeneration of canopy tree species since about 1970, which coincides with the initiation of the deer population irruption. A number of herbs and shrubs have been greatly reduced in the understory, and their propagules from the soil.

Deer do not readily transmit the bacterium that causes Lyme disease to other organisms, but deer are important hosts for adult ticks which underscores their importance in the transmission pathway of the disease to humans. Deer on FIIS, while occasionally docile, are still wild animals and should be treated as such. Some animals are relatively unafraid of humans due to the absence of predation and a lack of harassment. This in turn has contributed to a long-standing tradition of feeding deer by many residents and visitors, particularly in western portions of the island. Feeding affects both the behavior and population dynamics of deer inhabiting Fire Island. Recent efforts to reduce deer feeding by visitors and residents have been very effective. Ongoing experiments with Porcine Zona Pellucida immunocontraception demonstrate some promise of this technology as a population management tool. Success appears to be linked directly to factors affecting access to deer, which vary considerably among treatment locations. Continued high National Park Service visibility among communities in the form of interpretive programs, extension and outreach activities, and continued support of research and monitoring of deer and their effects on island biota are keys to successful resolution of persistent issues.

Preface prepared by:
Charles T. Roman
National Park Service
North Atlantic Coast Cooperative Ecosystem Studies Unit

TABLE OF CONTENTS

SUMMARY

Lyme disease is the most common vector-borne disease on Fire Island. The Lyme spirochete, *Borrelia burgdorferi*, is endemic in local tick and wildlife populations. Public education, personal precautions against tick bite, and prompt treatment of early-stage infections can help manage the risk of Lyme disease on Fire Island. The pathogens that cause Human Monocytic Ehrlichiosis and Tularemia have been isolated from ticks or wildlife on Fire Island, and conditions suggest that other tick-borne diseases (including Babesiosis, Rocky Mountain Spotted Fever, and Human Granulocytic Ehrlichiosis) might also occur, but these are far less common than Lyme disease, if present.

West Nile Virus is the primary mosquito-borne human pathogen that is known to occur on Fire Island. Ecological conditions and recent epizootiological events suggest that WNV occurs in foci that can shift from year to year. Therefore, a surveillance program with appropriate responses to increasing epizootic activity can help manage the risk of WNV transmission on Fire Island.

INTRODUCTION

Several vector-borne disease agents are known to occur on Fire Island (FIIS), including both tick-borne and mosquito-borne pathogens. Ginsberg (1990) reviewed the vector-borne diseases of FIIS and concluded that Lyme disease was the most common, with mosquito-borne arbovirusal diseases being rare or absent. The recent introduction of West Nile Virus (WNV) to the New York area has modified this situation, and requires renewed attention. In this review, the occurrence of eleven tick-borne and five mosquito-borne pathogens (Tables 1 & 2) will be discussed. Some of these pathogens are known to occur at FIIS, while others could potentially occur. The potential for future occurrence, and ecological factors that influence occurrence, are assessed for each disease.

BACKGROUND

In this section, I review literature on tick-borne and mosquito-borne diseases that occur, or that might potentially occur, on Fire Island. Transmission of human diseases by other blood-feeding arthropods on Fire Island (lice, fleas, biting midges, etc.) has not been reported.

The discussion in this report requires the use of several entomological and medical terms. Most of the diseases covered are **zoonotic diseases** or **zoonoses**, which means that they are primarily diseases of animals (which can sometimes be transmitted to people). This report covers only **vector-borne diseases**, which are diseases transmitted by **vectors**, most commonly arthropods such as ticks or mosquitoes. Vertebrates that maintain the pathogen are called **reservoirs**. The pathogen persists in populations of reservoirs, and is transmitted to other vertebrates, including other reservoirs, and sometimes humans, by vectors. The maintenance of pathogens in wild animals, and transmission by vectors, is the **enzootic cycle**. When enzootic spread increases substantially, this increase is called **epizootic** activity. If the pathogen is transmitted to humans, this is **epidemic** activity. For many diseases, the vectors responsible for enzootic transmission are the same species as for epidemic transmission (e.g., Lyme disease). In contrast, for some pathogens different vector species are involved in enzootic transmission than in transmission to people. In this case, **enzootic vectors** can be distinguished from **epidemic vectors** or **bridge vectors** (vectors that bridge the cycle from enzootic to epidemic activity). An example is West Nile Virus in the northeast, where enzootic transmission occurs among birds by bird-feeding mosquitoes, while epidemic activity involves mosquitoes with broader host ranges that bite both birds (where they can acquire the virus) and mammals (to which they can later transmit the pathogen). The pathogen that causes a disease is called the **etiologic agent** of the disease. **Prevalence** is the proportion of a group of organisms at a given time that are infected with a pathogen, expressed as a proportion or percentage. **Incidence**, on the other hand, is the number of new infections per unit time. Thus prevalence is a proportion, while incidence is a rate. For comprehensive background information, the reader is referred to Mullen & Durden (2002)..

Tick-Borne Diseases

Ticks are Arachnids, related to other eight-legged arthropods such as mites, spiders, and scorpions. The ticks associated with disease transmission to humans on Fire Island are hard ticks, family Ixodidae. The three species that most commonly bite humans include the black-legged tick or deer tick, *Ixodes scapularis*, the American dog tick, *Dermacentor variabilis*, and the Lone star tick, *Amblyomma americanum*. These species hatch from the eggs as larvae (which have six legs), attach to a vertebrate host, engorge with blood, then drop off and molt to the nymphal stage. The nymphs attach to hosts, engorge, drop off, then molt to the adult stage (nymphs and adults have eight legs). Adults mate, take blood meals, and the females lay eggs. This life cycle typically takes two years on Fire Island. Pathogens can be picked up during feeding on vertebrate hosts during any stage of the life cycle. Pathogens that are acquired during the larval or nymphal stages can be transmitted horizontally to vertebrate hosts during nymphal or adult feeding. In some cases (e.g., Rocky Mountain Spotted Fever), pathogens can be transmitted vertically from female ticks directly to their offspring. Details of tick biology and disease transmission are covered by Sonenshine (1991, 1993).

Powassan Encephalitis

Powassan virus has been isolated from several species of ixodid ticks in New York State. Traditionally, the primary vector was considered to be *Ixodes cookei*, which attaches primarily to woodchucks (not known from Fire Island) and carnivores (Artsob 1989, Kierans & Litwak 1989). Powassan virus can cause severe encephalitis in people, but human cases are rare. Recently, a new flavivirus in the Tick-Borne-Encphalitis group was isolated from deer ticks, *Ixodes scapularis* (=*I. dammini*), in coastal New England (Telford et al. 1997). This virus, which is currently called deer tick virus (DTV), has been isolated from *I. scapularis* and from white-footed mice, *Peromyscus leucopus*, in New England and Wisconsin (Ebel et al. 1999, 2000).

DTV is currently considered a lineage of Powassan virus (Ebel et al. 2001), but it is not clear whether it causes human disease.

Red fox (*Vulpes fulva*) are present on Fire Island (Northup 1985), so *I. cookei* could also be present (although this species has not been reported on FIIS). *I. scapularis* and *P. leucopus* are common on Fire Island (Ginsberg 1992), so DTV could potentially occur as well. However, to date no Powassan virus strains have been recorded on Fire Island.

Rocky Mountain Spotted Fever (RMSF)

The American dog tick, *Dermacentor variabilis*, is the primary vector of the etiologic agent of RMSF, *Rickettsia rickettsii*, in the eastern United States (Harwood & James 1979). Nationwide, the number of human cases varies from roughly 200 to 1200 per year, with most cases in the southeastern and southcentral states (Burgdorfer 1975, CDC 1990). New York state averaged 10.8 cases per year from 1997 through 2001 (CDC 1998, 1999, 2001a, 2002a, 2003). *D. variabilis* infected with *R. rickettsii* is widely distributed on Long Island (Benach et al. 1977), and human cases of RMSF have been reported (Vianna & Hinman 1971, White & Flynn 1990). However, no cases have been specifically attributed to tick bites on Fire Island, partly because frequent travel between Fire Island and Long Island makes it difficult to pinpoint the site where an infection was acquired. The lone star tick, *A. americanum*, has been suspected as a vector of RMSF, but this remains controversial, and current thought is that this is highly unlikely.

Both *D. variabilis* and *A. americanum* occur on Fire Island (Ginsberg 1992*).* R. rickettsii* is transmitted vertically (from mother to offspring) by *D. variabilis*, and some wildlife species can apparently function as reservoirs to amplify infection. Species that can potentially serve as reservoirs on Fire Island include eastern cottontail rabbits (*Sylvilagus floridanus*), and several species of rodents, medium-sized mammals, and birds (Burgdorfer 1975, McCormick 1975, Northup 1985). Therefore, ecological conditions are such that RMSF could be present on Fire Island. The primary vector, *D. variabilis*, is far less common that either *I. scapularus* or *A. americanum*, and if it exists, RMSF is far less common than Lyme disease on Fire Island. Nevertheless, the focal nature of *D. variabilis* distribution could potentially result in local hotspots of infection that might not be easily detected by routine sampling. Therefore, precautions against possible exposure to RMSF should be maintained, especially in view of the severity of the infection.

Human Granulocytic Ehrlichiosis (HGE)

Anaplasma phagocytophilum (formerly *Ehrlichia phagocytophila*) was first isolated from ticks and from human patients in the northern Midwest in the 1990's (Chen et al. 1994, Dumler et al. 2001). The primary vector is the black-legged tick (=deer tick), *Ixodes scapularis*, and its mammal hosts serve as reservoirs, especially the white-footed mouse, *Peromyscus leucopus* (Pancholi et al. 1995, Levin & Fish 2001). This rickettsial pathogen causes a febrile illness of varying severity in people, and can sometimes be fatal.

The distribution of *A. phagocytophilum* in North America is now known to include the Atlantic coastal states, the northern Midwest, and California (CDC 2003, Maurin et al. 2003). In New York State, ehrlichiosis (including HGE and HME) has been reported from the lower Hudson Valley area and from eastern Long Island (CDC 1998, Wallace et al. 1998, Aguero-Rosenfeld 2002). A total of 241 cases of HGE were reported to the CDC from New York state in 1999, 2000, and 2001 (CDC 2001a, 2002a, 2003). There have been few or no attempts to isolate *A. phagocytophilum* from ticks on Fire Island, but since the vector and reservoir are both common on FIIS the pathogen could potentially exist there as well. Whether *A. phagocytophilum* occurs on Fire Island is currently unknown.

Human Monocytic Ehrlichiosis (HME)

Ehrlichia chaffeensis was first isolated from patients and ticks in the late 1980's (Anderson et al. 1991). The pathogen, which causes a febrile illness of varying severity that can sometimes be fatal, is now known to be widely distributed in the United States (CDC 1998, 2003, Paddock & Childs 2003). A total of 35 cases of HME were reported from New York state in 1999, 2000, and 2001 (CDC 2001a, 2002a, 2003). The primary vector is the lone star tick, *Amblyomma americanum*, and the primary vertebrate reservoir is the white-tailed deer, *Odocoileus virginianus* (Ewing et al. 1995). Both species are highly abundant on Fire Island (Ginsberg & Zhioua 1996, 1999, Underwood et al. 1998). The lone star tick, formerly a southern species with dense populations known from the New Jersey pine barrens and south (Hair & Bowman 1986), is expanding its range northward, and is now abundant on Fire Island, eastern Long Island, NY, and on Prudence Island in Narragansett Bay, RI (Ginsberg et al. 1991, Mather & Mather 1990).

Recently, *I. chaffeensis* was isolated from *A. americanum* collected at the Lighthouse Tract on Fire Island (Mixson et al. 2004). Infection rates were low, with 5.4 % of adults (N=37), and less than 1 % of nymphs (N=221) infected. Further sampling is currently underway to assess the distribution and prevalence of *I. chaffeensis* in lone star ticks on Fire Island and southern Long Island, and the pathogen has now been isolated from several sites in eastern Long Island (this is a collaborative effort including the National Park Service, U.S. Geological Survey, Centers for Disease Control, Suffolk County Vector Control, and the University of Rhode Island).

Human Ehrlichiosis

Ehrlichia ewingii has been isolated from dogs in New York State (Goodman et al. 2003), and can cause disease in humans as well, especially immunocompromised patients (Sonenshine et al. 2002). *E. ewingii* can be transmitted by *A. americanum*, but it is not known whether this pathogen occurs on Fire Island.

Table 1. Tick-borne diseases that are present, or that could potentially occur on Fire Island.

Pathogen	Disease	Primary Vectors*	Isolated from Fire Island[†]
Deer Tick Virus	Powassan Encephalitis	Ixodes scapularis	No
Rickettsia rickettsii	Rocky Mountain Spotted Fever	Dermacentor variabilis	No
Anaplasma phagocytophilum	Human Granulocytic Ehrlichiosis	Ixodes scapularis	No
Ehrlichia chaffeensis	Human Monocytic Ehrlichiosis	Amblyomma americanum	Yes
Ehrlichia ewingii	Human ehrlichiosis	Amblyomma americanum	No
Borrelia burgdorferi	Lyme disease (Lyme borreliosis)	Ixodes scapularis	Yes
Borrelia lonestari	Lyme disease-like syndrome ?	Amblyomma americanum	No
Borrelia sp. nov. (relapsing fever group)	unknown	Ixodes scapularis	No
Francisella tularensis	Tularemia	ixodid tick species (or contact with rabbit)	Yes
Coxiella burnetii	Q Fever	airborne transmission, various tick species	No
Babesia microti	Babesiosis	Ixodes scapularis	No

*   All tick species listed have been collected on Fire Island (Ginsberg 1992).

[†]   Pathogen has been isolated from tick or from wild vertebrate host on Fire Island (see text for details).

Table 2. Mosquito-borne diseases that are present, or that could potentially occur on Fire Island.

Pathogen/Disease	Enzootic Vector(s)*	Potential Bridge Vectors*	Isolated[†]
West Nile Virus	*Culex pipiens* *Cx. restuans*	*Cx. salinarius* *Aedes vexans* *Aedes sollicitans* *Coquillettidia perturbans*	Yes
St. Louis Encephalitis	*Cx. pipiens*		No
Eastern Equine Encephalitis	*Culiseta melanura*	*Ae. vexans* *Ae. sollicitans* *Cq. Perturbans*	No
LaCrosse Encephlaitis	*Ae. triseriatus*	*Ae. triseriatus*	?
Malaria	not zoonotic	*Anopheles quadrimaculatus* *An. Punctipennis*	No

* All mosquito species listed have been collected on Fire Island (Ginsberg & Rohlf 1985, Lussier 2003).

† Pathogen has been isolated from mosquito or from wild vertebrate host on Fire Island (see text for detai

6

Lyme disease (LD, Lyme borreliosis)

Lyme disease is the most commonly reported tick-borne disease in the United States. Reported cases each year were in the 16,000 - 17,000 range nationwide in the late 1990's through 2001, but climbed to 23,763 cases in 2002 (CDC 2004). Human cases are mostly concentrated in the northeastern, mid-Atlantic, and north central states (CDC 2001b, 2003). From 1991 through 2001, New York state averaged 4,172 human cases per year (CDC 1992, 1993, 1994, 1995, 1996, 1997, 1998, 1999, 2001a, 2002a, 2003), with LD activity concentrated in eastern Long Island and the lower Hudson River valley (White 1991). Of national park sites in the eastern U.S., Fire Island has the highest density of deer ticks, *Ixodes scapularis*, infected with the Lyme disease spirochete, *Borrelia burgdorferi* (Ginsberg 1992). Lyme disease is common on Fire Island, which has been the subject of epidemiological studies of Lyme disease (Hanrahan et al. 1984) as well as numerous studies of tick ecology (Ginsberg & Ewing 1989, Ginsberg & Zhioua 1996, 1999, Ginsberg et al. 1998, Zhioua et al. 1999) and spirochete transmission dynamics (Ginsberg 1988, 1992, 1993a).

The high prevalence of Lyme disease results from the abundance of excellent reservoir species (e.g., white-footed mice, *Peromyscus leucopus*), coupled with the abundance of vectors (*Ixodes scapularis*), and the two-year life cycle of the vector (Lane et al. 1991, Ginsberg 1992, 1993b, Piesman 2002). Eggs hatch in mid summer, and the largely uninfected larvae attach to small mammal and bird hosts, where they can acquire the pathogen. These larvae overwinter and emerge as nymphs the following spring, and many of the nymphs are infected. They feed and emerge as adults in the fall, with a higher prevalence of infection in adults than in nymphs. However, since the nymphs are active during peak periods of human activity (May through July), most human cases result from the bites of nymphal ticks (Fish 1993).

Management of ticks and Lyme disease has been reviewed by several authors (e.g., Wilson & Deblinger 1993, Stafford & Kitron 2002, Ginsberg & Stafford in press). However, because of the high prevalence of *B. burgdorferi* in high-density tick populations on Fire Island, routine management is unlikely to interrupt the enzootic cycle (Ginsberg 1992, 1993a). Specific recommendations for personal protection against tick bite on Fire Island have been developed (Ginsberg 1990, 1992), and remain important. A vaccine that was formerly available against Lyme disease (Hayes & Schriefer 2002), has been removed from the market by the manufacturer.

Borrelia lonestari (Lyme disease-like syndrome)

Early reports suggested that the lone star tick, *A. americanuim*, could transmit Lyme disease (Schulze et al. 1984). However, the spirochete isolated *from A. americanum*, though positive in some relatively non-specific immunological tests, could not be cultured in BSK medium, the standard method for *B. burgdorferi*. Subsequent study has identified a new spirochete from *A. americanum* (Barbour et al. 1996), which has been named *Borrelia lonestari*. This spirochete might be responsible for a Lyme-like syndrome found in some patients bitten by lone star ticks (James et al. 1996), but this has not been definitively established. Lone star ticks have been screened for spirochetes on Fire Island, including 52 nymphs, 3 adult males and 2 females collected by flagging and analyzed by dark field microscopy (Ginsberg 1992), and 260 nymphs collected as they dropped as engorged larvae from birds that were collected in mistnets at the Lighthouse Tract on Fire Island and tested by Direct Immunofluorescent Assay (DFA) using a fluorescein isothiocyanate conjugated goat antibody to *B. burgdorferi* (Kierkegaard & Perry Laboratories, Gaithersburg, MD) (Balmforth 2002). None of these lone star ticks (total = 317) were positive for *Borrelia*.

Relapsing fever group *Borrelia*

A new species of *Borrelia* was recently isolated from ticks that engorged on *Borrelia burgdorferi*-infected mice (Scoles et al. 2001). This spirochete was positive using the standard DFA technique (Kirkegaard & Perry Laboratories, Gaithersburg, MD) commonly used to test ticks for infection with *B. burgdorferi*. Therefore, many ticks that are DFA-positive for the Lyme disease spirochete, *B. burgdorferi*, are in fact infected by this new species of *Borrelia*.

The new *Borrelia* species is in the relapsing fever group (not the Lyme borreliosis group) and is most closely related to the Japanese species *B. miyamotoi* (Scoles et al. 2001). A collection of 160 nymphal *I. scapularis* from Westchester County, NY, yielded 17 nymphs positive for *B. burgdorferi* and 4 positive for the new *Borrelia* species. Similar results were obtained in Rhode Island, Connecticut, and New Jersey, but the new *Borrelia* was not found in a collection of *I. scapularis* from Maryland (Scoles et al. 2001).

Borrelia burgdorferi-positive ticks on Fire Island have been tested by DFA, IFA, and dark field microscopy, which are relatively non-specific tests. Therefore, some of the positives could actually have been this new species of *Borrelia*. It is not known whether this *Borrelia* sp. causes illness in humans. Ticks collected from vertebrates on Fire Island are currently being tested for infection with this spirochete.

Tularemia

Tularemia, sometimes called Rabbit fever, is caused by the bacterium *Francisella tularensis*, and is carried by Eastern cottontail rabbits (*Sylvilagus floridanus*) in the northeastern U.S. The pathogen can be transmitted to humans via tick bite, by the bite of bloodfeeding insects (e.g., tabanid flies), or directly from diseased rabbits by contact with infected fluids or aerosols (Harwood & James 1979). Tick bite is apparently a common mode of transmission in the western states, while direct contact of hunters with rabbits during skinning is the primary means of transmission in the eastern U.S.

Tularemia is uncommon in New York State, with the number of reported cases ranging from zero to two per year (mean = 1 per year, data from 1990-1994, and 2000-2001) (CDC 1991, 1992, 1993, 1994, 1995, 2002a, 2003). Ticks that have been implicated in transmission of tularemia (*D. variabilis, A. americanum*, and *Haemaphysalis leporispalustris*) occur on Fire Island, and *F. tularensis* was detected by the USFWS Pathology Lab in Madison, WI in a cottontail that was found dead on Fire Island in 1983 (Northup 1985). Therefore, tularemia can be contracted on Fire Island, but there have been no cases attributed to tick bite, and the primary risk is to rabbit hunters handling the cottontails that they hunt.

Q Fever

Q Fever is caused by the bacterium *Coxiella burnetii*, which is widely distributed in the United States in domestic and wild animals (McQuiston & Childs 2002). Transmission to humans typically results from direct contact with infected sheep or goats, but transmission by tick bite can also occur. It is not known whether *C. burnetii* occurs on Fire Island.

Babesiosis

Babesiosis, caused by the protozoan pathogen, *Babesia microti*, causes a malaria-like illness in coastal areas of New York and New England (Dammin et al. 1981, Spielman et al. 1985). The natural reservoirs are rodents (especially the white-footed mouse, *P. leucopus*), and the primary vector is *I. scapularis* (Spielman 1976, Spielman et al. 1979). This pathogen has been reported from eastern Long Island (Benach et al. 1978, Bosler & Schulze 1987) and human cases have been reported from Davis Park on Fire Island (J.L. Benach, NY State Dept. Health, personal communication). In view of the abundance of vectors and reservoirs, and the presence of human cases, babesiosis clearly occurs on Fire Island, but the degree of human risk has not been assessed.

Mosquito-Borne Diseases

Mosquitoes are flies, order Diptera, in the family Culicidae. Eggs are laid directly on water (e.g., genus *Culex*) or on surfaces that will later be flooded (e.g., genus *Aedes*). In this report, I use the genus name *Aedes* (rather than *Ochlerotatus* for some species), following the editorial policy of the *Journal of Medical Entomology* (2005). Larvae hatch from the eggs and are aquatic filter feeders. They breathe air through terminal siphons. Larvae go through four instars (the stages between molts) as larvae, then pupate. Pupae are also aquatic, and though they do not feed, they are active and will wriggle if disturbed. After emerging from the pupal exoskeleton, adults live in aerial and terrestrial environments. They typically mate, find nectar meals, sometimes migrate, and then seek hosts. Only females bite vertebrates to obtain blood, which is necessary for proteins and lipids for egg development. After digestion of the blood meal and development of eggs, females seek oviposition sites. After oviposition, they seek additional blood meals. A single female mosquito can go through several cycles of blood feeding and oviposition in her life. Pathogens are typically acquired in an early feeding, then transmitted during a later feeding episode. In some cases, pathogens can be transmitted vertically from mother to offspring (e.g., vertical transmission of LaCrosse Encephalitis virus by *Aedes triseriatus*). Additional background material is presented by Mullen & Durden (2002) and by Service (1993).

West Nile Encephalitis (caused by West Nile Virus, WNV)

WNV was first detected in the Western Hemisphere in 1999, when 62 cases of West Nile Encephalitis (resulting in 7 deaths) were reported in northern Queens, in New York City. The virus has since spread throughout most of the continental United States (CDC 2002b), and also to Mexico and other countries in Central America, as well as to Canada. In 2003, there were 9,862 recorded cases (with 264 deaths) in the U.S. (see CDC website: www.cdc.gov). Originally, WNV existed in Africa and the Mediterranean regions of Asia and Europe, with occasional outbreaks in central Europe, Russia, and sub-Saharan Africa (Komar 2000). The strain that was transported to the U.S. in 1999 is genetically similar to strains found in Israel and Egypt (Lanciotti et al. 1999). WNV typically does not cause illness in wild birds in the Old World, but it does affect several North American species with substantial mortality in some corvids (especially crows and blue jays) and some raptors. WNV infections cause no symptoms or only minor symptoms in most people, with only about one in 150 infected people showing symptoms, and with most severe cases (including encephalitis with long term sequelae) in elderly patients.

WNV is maintained in the northeast in an enzootic cycle including birds as reservoirs, and the mosquitoes *Culex pipiens* and *Cx. restuans* (both primarily ornithophilic species) as the enzootic vectors (Kulasekera et al. 2001). These mosquito species are competent vectors in lab trials (Turrell et al. 2001, Sardelis et al. 2001, Goddard et al. 2002). The proportion of mosquitoes ingesting infected blood that later shed virus in their saliva under lab conditions (= estimated transmission rate, ETR) was 20% for *Cx. pipiens* and 55% for *Cx. restuans* (Turrell 2001, Sardelis et al. 2001). The larvae of both species are commonly found in artificial containers (Means 1987), so these mosquitoes are abundant in urban areas. Birds that are competent reservoirs include many species that are common in areas with dense human populations, such as crows, blue jays, robins, house sparrows, and others (Komar et al. 2003). Since both reservoir bird species and bird-feeding mosquito vector species are common in urban areas, the enzootic cycle of this virus can build to epizootic levels in areas with high density human populations. When large numbers of birds are infective, vector-competent mosquitoes that have broad host ranges, can feed on infective birds (picking up the virus) and later bite humans. These mosquitoes can act as bridge vectors (serving as a bridge from the enzootic cycle to humans), sometimes called "epidemic" vectors. The primary bridge vector species in the northeast is apparently *Cx. salinarius* (Kulasekera et al. 2001), but other species can potentially play this role, including *Aedes sollicitans* and *Aedes vexans*. In laboratory trials, *Cx. salinarius* showed high vector competence (ETR = 34%), *Ae. sollicitans* showed low to moderate vector competence (ETR = 11%), and *Ae. vexans* showed modest vector competence (ETR = 8%) (Turrell et al. 2001, Sardelis et al. 2001).

All of these five mosquito species are common on Fire Island (Ginsberg & Rohlf 1985, Lussier 2003), as are several reservoir competent bird species. Therefore. conditions exist for WNV activity at FIIS. In fact, mosquitoes positive for WNV have been collected at Saltaire and Cherry Grove (Suffolk County Vector Control, pers comm), at the western portion of Watch Hill near Davis Park, and recently at the William Floyd Estate (2001 - 2003, FIIS mosquito/WNV surveillance). Ecological conditions are appropriate for WNV activity, and the virus has been found in mosquitoes on Fire Island, so appropriate surveillance and management programs are indicated.

St. Louis Encephalitis (SLE)

SLE is a flavivirus in the Japanese Encephalitis Group (which includes WNV), and was the only member of that group in the New World before the introduction of WNV. The ecology of SLE is similar to that of WNV, and it exists in a bird-mosquito cycle with similar vector species (Harwood & James 1979). Therefore, though it is rare most years, SLE sometimes causes substantial disease outbreaks, often in large cities (Tsai & Mitchell 1989). Human cases of SLE were reported in New York state in the 1970's (Ginsberg 1990), but SLE is rare in New York, and there were no human cases from 1998 through 2001 (CDC 1999, 2001a, 2002, 2003). Although SLE could theoretically occur on FIIS, it has not been reported from Fire Island and it is far more common in the southern, midwestern and western states.

Eastern Equine Encephalitis (EEE)

EEE is an extremely severe disease, with mortality of human cases in the 50% range, and roughly half of the surviving patients with long term neurological deficits (Tsai & Monath 1987, Morris 1988). Fortunately, it is quite rare, with an average of about 5 human cases per year, nationwide (CDC 2003). The enzootic transmission cycle of EEE virus involves mosquito vectors and bird reservoirs. Unlike WNV, however, the primary enzootic vector is *Culiseta melanura* (Chamberlain 1958, Jamnback et al. 1965), which breeds in freshwater swamps and not in urban areas. Therefore, the enzootic cycle of EEE virus occurs in swamp habitat, not near human population centers. For EEE virus to infect humans, a buildup to epizootic levels in birds must occur in swamps at the same time that large populations of potential bridge vectors are present. Potential bird reservoirs include such species as robins, catbirds, and possibly yellow-shafted flickers (Bast et al. 1973, Srihonge et al. 1980). Possible bridge vector mosquito species include *Coquillettidia perturbans* (Boromisa et al. 1987), *Ae. sollicitans* (Crans 1977), and *Ae. vexans* (Wallis et al. 1960). The bridge vectors must pick up the infection, then during a subsequent blood meal either bite a person who has entered the swamp, or leave the swamp habitat and bite a person elsewhere. This requirement for several factors to occur at the same time, in sites distant from human population centers, explains to a large extent why EEE is so rare in people.

The enzootic and bridge vector species occur on Fire Island, but the enzootic vector, *Cs. melanura*, has rarely been collected. The freshwater swamp habitat of this species is found in the Sunken Forest. In a joint NPS/CDC surveillance program in 1983-1985, a total of 34,928 mosquitoes were tested for EEE. None were positive. Only 3 *Cs. melanura* were collected, all at the Sunken Forest. In contrast, populations of the most common potential bridge vector species, *Ae. sollicitans*, are highest at the east end of Fire Island where the salt marsh habitat of this species is common, several km east of the Sunken Forest. Therefore, the results of the NPS/CDC surveillance program suggested that ecological conditions on Fire Island were not conducive to human risk of EEE infection. In fact, EEE has never been isolated on Fire Island, and there have been no confirmed human cases of EEE on Fire Island or on Long Island (CDC 1999, 2001a, 2002a, 2003, McGowan et al. 1973, Morris et al. 1973, Zaki 1979).

EEE has occurred in domestic animals such as horses on Long Island (Bast et al. 1973). Also, EEE activity has been detected in *Cs. melanura* in swamps along the Carmans River, several miles north of Smith Point (Jamnback et al. 1965*). Ae. sollicitans* emerging at the Hospital Point salt marsh on Fire Island seek blood meals along Fire Island, and a small percentage move to Long Island, where they are abundant in southern Shirley within about 0.8 mi of Smith Point (Ginsberg & Rohlf 1985, Ginsberg 1986). These mosquitoes disperse into the Mastic-Shirley area, and many undoubtedly eventually reach the swamp areas along the Carmans River where EEE activity has been reported. Above the southern 0.8 mi area they do not predominate, and are mixed with mosquitoes from numerous source areas (Ginsberg & Rohlf 1985). Nevertheless, surveillance to detect this possibility is appropriate.

Finally, small populations of *Cs. melanura* at the Sunken Forest are unlikely to result in epizootic activity in local birds. However, if *Cs. melanura* populations were to increase substantially, epizootic activity would be possible. If a potential bridge vector (e.g., *Ae. vexans*) was abundant at the time, transmission to mammals could potentially occur. Unlikely thought this scenario might be, surveillance in the Sunken Forest area is appropriate. If *Cs. melanura* populations were to increase substantially, then additional surveillance, including testing of mosquitoes for EEE virus, would be indicated.

LaCrosse Encephalitis (LAC)

LAC virus is the most common of several strains of California Group Encephalitis (CGE) viruses, most of which do not cause illness in humans (LeDuc 1987). LAC (which was named after LaCrosse, WI) is most common in the upper midwestern states (Grimstad 1988). The primary reservoirs are mammals, and the primary vector is *Ae. triseriatus*, a cavity-dwelling mosquito species that commonly breeds in discarded tires (Means 1979). The virus is passed vertically from mother to offspring mosquitoes. *Ae. triseriatus* is present on Long Island (Guirgis & Sanzone 1978), but human cases of LAC encephalitis are rare in New York, and none were reported from 1998 through 2001 (CDC 1999, 2001a, 2002a, 2003). The NPS/CDC surveillance program in 1983-1985 yielded one pool of *Ae. sollicitans* positive for a strain of CGE virus, but the strain was not identified. The relative rarity of *Ae. triseriatus* on Fire Island (Lussier 2003), and the lack of piles of discarded tires, argue against the likelihood of LAC becoming a problem on Fire Island.

Cache Valley Virus

Cache Valley Virus is a bunyavirus associated with fetal death in sheep and other animals in North America (Calisher et al. 1986). It rarely affects humans, but a few cases of human illness associated with infection have been reported. A Bunyamwera group virus, probably Cache Valley Virus, was isolated by the New York State Department of Health lab from a pool of *Ae. sollicitans* from Fire Island collected in September 1993 (M. Lawrence, pers. comm.). This virus has occasionally been isolated from Suffolk County, NY, in previous years.

Malaria

Malaria is the most common parasitic disease of tropical areas worldwide (Wernsdorfer & McGregor 1988), causing hundreds of millions of cases and roughly two million deaths each year (Martens & Hall 2000). It was formerly common in North America as well, including New York state, but has been largely eradicated by modification of wetland habitats (channelizing marsh and swamp habitats associated with larger bodies of water and converting natural wetlands into farm ponds), spraying mosquitoes with insecticides, and treating malaria patients. Malaria is caused by protozoa of the genus *Plasmodium* and is transmitted by mosquitoes of the genus *Anopheles* (Harwood & James 1979). Human malaria is not a zoonosis, but exists in a human-mosquito transmission cycle in the tropics. The major species that could act as vectors in the northeastern U.S. are *An. quadrimaculatus* and *An. punctipennis*. Both of these species are present, but are not common on Fire Island (Lussier 2003).

Since 1995, there have been 7 to 17 human cases of malaria each year in Suffolk County, virtually all imported (CDC 2000). Typically, visitors or immigrants from malarious parts of the world arrive with the infection, either before they show symptoms, or after they have recovered (some species of *Plasmodium* have stages that remain in the human liver while the patient is asymptomatic, and then cause relapses after long periods of time). On rare occasions, a person who was infected outside of the U.S. and then travels to North America is bitten by an *Anopheles* mosquito, which acquires the infection and later transmits it to humans in the U.S. This occurred on Long Island in 1999, resulting in 2 human cases of malaria acquired locally (CDC 2000). This type of local transmission occurs occasionally, but is rare in New York. The relative rarity of *An. quadrimaculatus* and *An. punctipennis* on Fire Island, suggest that while this scenario is possible, it is unlikely on the barrier island.

VECTOR-BORNE DISEASE MONITORING AT FIRE ISLAND NATIONAL SEASHORE

Tick-Borne Diseases

The park sponsored a "Lyme Fest" each August during several years in the 1980's, in which park staff had blood drawn for testing at Dr. R. Dattwyler's lab at SUNY Stony Brook for antibodies to Lyme disease spirochetes. Initial results showed park staff seroconverting at a rate of approximately 12 % each year. The park initiated a tick and Lyme disease awareness and precaution program, based on the results of a study of tick and spirochete distribution on the barrier island (Ginsberg 1990), and frequent talks by local experts (J. Benach, R. Dattwyler, H.S. Ginsberg), signage, and precautions instituted among park staff. Yearly seroconversion rates subsequently decreased substantially, and were near zero in most years. This decline apparently resulted partly from greater awareness and avoidance of tick bites, and partly from rapid recognition of Lyme symptoms by park staff, resulting in timely treatment of early-stage infections.

The effectiveness of the park's public education program (including displays, signage, and discussion in interpretive programs) on Lyme disease incidence in visitors to the park is not known, partly because of the difficulty in tracking visitors and in determining whether exposure to the ticks occurred on Fire Island or elsewhere.

Mosquito-Borne Diseases

A monitoring program for EEE was conducted by FIIS staff in conjunction with the CDC from 1983-1985. A total of 34,928 mosquitoes were tested, primarily *Ae. sollicitans*, and none were positive for EEE. One pool of *Ae. sollicitans* was positive for a California Group Virus, but the serotype was not determined. The California Group includes about a dozen serotypes, most of which do not cause illness in humans (LeDuc 1987). Since this initial program, and the publication of the concurrent mosquito dispersal study (Ginsberg & Rohlf 1985, Ginsberg 1986) there have been no pesticide applications for mosquito/EEE control at FIIS, and there have been no human cases of EEE.

Active monitoring resumed in 1998, with a plan that included mosquito population monitoring and EEE surveillance in trapped mosquitoes, with a graded management response to increasing levels of transmission risk. When WNV appeared in New York City in 1999, the plan was modified to include surveillance for WNV activity. The "Mosquito surveillance and management protocol" has been updated each year since, and the 2003 protocol is provided in Appendix 1. The park also produces a "Mosquito Action Plan" (MAP) each year, which provides detailed operational instructions for carrying out the protocol. The 2003 MAP is provided in Appendix 2.

Surveillance results are summarized after the mosquito season each year, and presented in a mosquito surveillance and management report. The 2003 report is provided in Appendix 3. Previous years' reports are available from the Resource Management office at FIIS.

RELATIONSHIPS WITH SUFFOLK COUNTY, NEW YORK STATE, AND FEDERAL AGENCIES

Fire Island National Seashore maintains active working relationships with Suffolk County Vector Control, the New York State Department of Health, the Centers for Disease Control, and the U.S. Geological Survey. The park's mosquito surveillance and management protocol was initially written by an expert from the USGS (Dr. H.S. Ginsberg) and completed with comments and modifications suggested by the National Park Service, CDC, New York State Department of Health, and Suffolk County Vector Control. The USGS scientist occasionally visits the park to provide training and to fine-tune the protocol. The park's mosquito surveillance and management program involves trapping and sorting of mosquitoes by park staff, and transporting of specimens to the Suffolk County Vector Control lab, where the mosquito pools are packed and shipped to the New York State Health Department lab in Albany, NY, for viral testing. The Suffolk County Vector Control entomologist, Dr. S.R. Campbell, interacts with the USGS scientist, and provides on-site consultation for park staff on practical matters related to mosquito surveillance.

Mosquito surveillance results (from trapping and larval sampling), and the results of viral testing, are available to the national seashore, Suffolk County Vector Control, and NY State Health Department. Results are also shared with appropriate experts from the USGS, who provide technical advice on surveillance and management. When surveillance suggests possible increasing risk of vector-borne disease transmission, a consultation process is initiated that includes the national seashore, Suffolk County Vector Control, and USGS experts. If further consultation is needed additional expertise is requested, including consultation with the CDC, Suffolk County Health Department, New York State Department of Health, etc.

Fire Island National Seashore maintains an active and congenial working relationship with Suffolk County Vector Control. Environmentally-benign larval management procedures, including sanitation of debris such as buckets and cups, manipulation of man-made containers that hold water, larval management in artificial containers, and maintenance of facilities to minimize artificial mosquito larval habitat, are actively performed by park staff. Also, an open marsh water management (OMWM) project was performed at the William Floyd Estate. This project was a cooperative effort between Suffolk County Vector Control, Fire Island National Seashore and others, and has apparently substantially reduced production of salt marsh mosquitoes (*Aedes sollicitans*) at the William Floyd Estate. However, because of the differing mandates of the two agencies, conflicts inevitably arise. Suffolk County Vector Control is charged with managing nuisance mosquito biting activity and arboviral disease transmission in Suffolk County, NY. Fire Island National Seashore is charged with preserving the natural resources of the National Seashore for the enjoyment of current and future generations. Therefore, interventions for mosquito control are restricted within FIIS to avoid negative effects on the natural systems in the park. Interventions that could adversely affect native species are permitted only when there is a clear risk to human health. Therefore, interventions (such as pesticide applications) that are routinely performed by Suffolk County Vector Control, are not permitted in the national seashore unless a public health threat is demonstrated. The park's mosquito surveillance and management protocol was designed to identify conditions under which there is a threat to human health, and which would call for active mosquito management within the national seashore. However, because of the complexity of the natural transmission cycles of mosquito-borne viruses, considerable interpretation of surveillance data is required to determine whether an imminent threat to human health exists. The consultation process established in the mosquito surveillance and management protocol is designed to promote discussion and mutually-agreed interpretation of surveillance results. Ultimately, the judgement on whether to allow pesticide applications within park boundaries lies with the park superintendent.

FUTURE CONSIDERATIONS

The vector borne disease with most human cases on Fire Island on a year-to-year basis is clearly Lyme disease. The Lyme spirochete is endemic in the tick and wildlife populations on

Fire Island, so the risk of human exposure is chronic. Public education, personal protection against tick bite, prompt medical attention for infected patients, and targeted interventions (e.g., landscaping to eliminate tick exposure around dwellings) can minimize the number of human cases.

Among mosquito-borne diseases, syndromes resulting from infection with WNV are most likely to cause human illness on Fire Island. Mosquitoes infected with WNV have been collected at Saltaire, Cherry Grove, near Watch Hill, and recently at the William Floyd Estate. In contrast to the endemic status of Lyme spirochetes, WNV apparently arises when ecological conditions are appropriate for viral amplification in birds and mosquitoes, and so its occurrence is focal and episodic. Therefore, management of WNV must be based on surveillance, with increasing levels of management in response to increasing levels of human disease risk. The mosquito surveillance and management protocols (Appendices 1 & 2) serve this function at present. In the future, our understanding of the transmission dynamics of WNV in this area, and of the relationship between epizootic activity and human disease, is expected to increase. The FIIS surveillance and management protocols should be updated with this new knowledge to more efficiently lower disease risk while protecting the natural resources of Fire Island National Seashore.

LITERATURE CITED

Aguero-Rosenfeld, M.E., L. Donnarumma, L. Zentmaier, J. Jacob, M. Frey, R. Noto, C.A. Carbonaro, & G.P. Wormser. 2002. Seroprevalence of antibodies that react with *Anaplasma phgocytophila*, the agent of Human Granulocytic Ehrlichiosis, in different populations in Westchester County, New York. *J. Clin. Microbiol.* **40**:2612-2615.

Anderson, B.E., J.E. Dawson, D.C. Jones & K.H. Wilson. 1991. *Ehrlichia chaffeensis*, a new species associated with human ehrlichiosis. *J. Clin. Microbiol.* **29**:2838-2842.

Artsob, H. 1989. Powassan encephalitis. pp. 29-49 *In:* T.P. Monath (ed.) *The Arboviruses: Epidemiology and Ecology, vol. IV.* CRC Press, Boca Raton, FL.

Balmforth, M.G. 2002. *Experimental examination of the reservoir competence of six species of native American songbirds for the Lyme disease pathogen, Borrelia burgdorferi*. Maser's Thesis, University of Rhode Island, Kingston, RI. 148 pp.

Barbour, A.G., G.O. Maupin, G.J. Tetlow, C.J. Carter, and J. Piesman. 1996. Identification of an uncultivable *Borrelia* species in the hard tick *Amblyomma americanum*: possible agent of a Lyme disease-like illness. *J. Infect. Dis.* **173**:403-409.

Bast, T.F., E. Whitney, & J.L. Benach. 1973. Considerations on the ecology of several arboviruses in eastern Long Island. *Am. J. Trop. Med. Hyg.* **22**:109-116.

Benach, J., D.J, White, W. Burgdorfer, T. Keelan, S. Guirgis, & R.H. Altieri. 1977. Changing patterns in the incidence of Rocky Mountain Spotted Fever on Long Island (1971-1976) *Am. J. Epidemiol* **106**:380-387..

Benach, J., D.J. White, & J.P. McGovern. 1978. Babesiosis on Long Island: host-parasite relationships of rodent and human-derived *Babesia microti* isolates in hamsters. *Am. J. Trop. Med. Hyg.* **27**:1073-1078.

Boromisa, R.D., R.S. Copeland, & P.R. Grimstad. 1987. Oral transmission of Eastern Equine Encephalomyelitis virus by a northern Indiana strain of *Coquillettidia perturbans*. *J. Am. Mosq. Ctrl. Assoc.* **3**:102-104.

Bosler, E.M. & T.L. Schulze. 1987. The prevalence and significance of *Borrelia burgdorferi* in the urine of feral reservoir hosts. *Zbl. Bakt. Hyg. A.* **263**:40-44.

Burgdorfer, W. 1975. A review of Rocky Mountain Spotted Fever (tick-borne typhus), its agent, and its tick vectors in the United States. *J. Med. Entomol.* **12**:269-278.

Calisher, C.H., D.B. Francy, G.C. Smith, D.J. Muth, J.S. Lazuick, N. Karabatsos, W.L. Jakob, & R.G. McLean. 1986. Distribution of Bunyamwera serogroup viruses in North America, 1956-1984. *Am. J. Trop. Med. Hyg.* **35**:429-443.

Chen, S.M., J.S. Dumler, J.S. Bakken, & D.H. Walker. 1994. Identification of a granulocytotropic *Ehrlichia* species as the etiologic agent of human disease. *J. Clin. Microbiol.* **32:**589-595.

CDC, Centers for Disease Control. 1990. Rocky Mountain Spotted Fever and human Ehrlichiosis - United States, 1989. *MMWR (Morbidity and Mortality Weekly Report)* **39:**281-284.

CDC, Centers for Disease Control. 1991. Summary of notifiable diseases, United States, 1990. *MMWR* **39(53):** 1-61.

CDC, Centers for Disease Control. 1992. Summary of notifiable diseases, United States, 1991. *MMWR* **40(53):** 1-63.

CDC, Centers for Disease Control. 1993. Summary of notifiable diseases, United States, 1992. *MMWR* **41(53):** 1-63.

CDC, Centers for Disease Control. 1994. Summary of notifiable diseases, United States, 1993. *MMWR* **42(53):** 1-73.

CDC, Centers for Disease Control. 1995. Summary of notifiable diseases, United States, 1994. *MMWR* **43(53):** 1-80.

CDC, Centers for Disease Control. 1996. Summary of notifiable diseases, United States, 1995. *MMWR* **44(53):** 1-87.

CDC, Centers for Disease Control. 1997. Summary of notifiable diseases, United States, 1996. *MMWR* **45(53):** 1-87.

CDC, Centers for Disease Control. 1998. Summary of notifiable diseases, United States, 1997. *MMWR* **46(54):** 1-87.

CDC, Centers for Disease Control. 1998. Statewide surveillance for ehrlichiosis –Connecticut and New York, 1994-1997. *MMWR* **47:**476-480.

CDC, Centers for Disease Control. 1999. Summary of notifiable diseases, United States, 1998. *MMWR* **47(53):** 1-93.

CDC, Centers for Disease Control. 2000. Probable locally acquired mosquito-transmitted *Plasmodium vivax* infection – Suffolk County, New York, 1999. *MMWR* **49:**495-498.

CDC, Centers for Disease Control. 2001a. Summary of notifiable diseases, United States, 1999. *MMWR* **48(53):** 1-104.

CDC, Centers for Disease Control. 2001b. Lyme disease – United States, 1999. *MMWR* **50:**181-5.

CDC, Centers for Disease Control. 2002a. Summary of notifiable diseases, United States, 2000. *MMWR* **49(53):** 1-102.

CDC, Centers for Disease Control. 2002b. Provisional surveillance summary of the West Nile Virus epidemic – United States, January-November 2002. *MMWR* **51:**1129-1133.

CDC, Centers for Disease Control. 2003. Summary of notifiable diseases, United States, 2001. *MMWR* **50(53):**1-136.

CDC, Centers for Disease Control. 2004. Lyme disease – United States, 2001-2002. *MMWR* **53(17):**365-369.

Chamberlain, R.W. 1958. Vector relationships of the arthropod-borne encephalitides in North America. *Ann. NY Acad. Sci.* **70:**312-319.

Crans, W.J. 1977. The status of *Aedes sollicitans* as an epidemic vector of eastern equine encephalitis in New Jersey. *Mosq. News* **37:**85-89.

Dammin, G.J., A. Spielman, J.L. Benach, & J. Piesman. 1981. The rising incidence of clinical *Babesia microti* infection. *Hum. Pathol.* **12:**398-400.

Dumler, J.S., A.F. Barbet, C.P. Bekker, G.A. Dasch, G.H. Palmer, S.C. Ray, Y. Rikihisa, & F.R. Rurangirwa. 2001. Reorganization of genera in the families Rickettsiaceae and Anaplasmataceae in the order Rickettsiales: unification of some species of *Ehrlichia* with *Anaplasma*, *Cowdria* with *Ehrlichia*, and *Ehrlichia* with *Neorickettsia*, descriptions of six new species combinations and designation of *Ehrlichia equi* and 'HGE agent' subjective synonyms of *Ehrlichia phagocytophila*. *Int. J. Syst. Evol, Microbiol.* **51:**2145-2165.

Ebel, G.D., E.N. Campbell, H.K. Goethert, A. Spielman, & S.R. Telford, 3rd. 2000. Enzootic transmission of deer tick virus in New England and Wisconsin sites. *Am. J. Trop. Med. Hyg.* **63:**36-42.

Ebel, G.D., I. Foppa, A. Spielman, & S.R. Telford, 3rd. 1999. A focus of deer tick virus transmission in the northcentral United States. *Emerg. Infect. Dis.* **5:**570-574.

Ebel, G.D., A. Spielman, & S.R. Telford, 3rd. 2001. Phylogeny of North American Powassan virus. *J. Gen. Virol.* **82:**1657-1665.

Editors. 2005. Journal policy on names of Aedine mosquito genera and subgenera. *J. Med. Entomol.* **42:**511.

Ewing, S.A., J.E. Dawson, A.A. Kocan, R.W. Barker, C.K. Warner, R.J. Panciera, J.C. Fox, K.M. Kocan & E.F. Blouin. 1995. Experimental transmission of *Ehrlichia chaffeensis* (Rickettsiales: Ehrlichiaceae) among white-tailed deer *by Amblyomma americanum* (Acari: Ixodidae). *J. Med. Entomol.* **32:**368-374.

Fish, D. 1993. Population ecology of *Ixodes dammini*. pp. 25-42 In. H.S. Ginsberg (ed.) *Ecology and Environmental Management of Lyme Disease*. Rutgers University Press. New Brunswick, NJ.

Ginsberg, H.S. 1986. Dispersal patterns of *Aedes sollicitans* (Diptera: Culicidae) at theeast end of Fire Island National Seashore, New York, USA *Journal of Medical Entomology* **23**:146-155.

Ginsberg, H.S. 1990. *Ecology and Management of Ticks and Lyme disease at FireIsland National Seashore and Selected Eastern National Parks*. National ParkService, North Atlantic Region, Report No. **OSS 90-1**. 170 pp.

Ginsberg, H.S. 1992. *Ecology and Management of Ticks and Lyme disease at Fire Island National Seashore and Selected Eastern National Parks*. National Park Service Scientific Monograph NPS/NRSUNJ/NRSM-92/20. 77 pp.

Ginsberg, H.S. 1993a. Transmission risk of Lyme disease and implications for tick management. *Am. J. Epidemiol.* **138**:65-73.

Ginsberg, H.S. (ed.) 1993b. *Ecology and Environmental Management of Lyme Disease*. Rutgers University Press. New Brunswick, NJ. 224 pp.

Ginsberg, H.S. and C.P. Ewing. 1989. Habitat distribution of *Ixodes dammini* (Acari:Ixodidae) and Lyme disease spirochetes on Fire Island, NY. *J. Med. Entomol.* **26**:183-189.

Ginsberg, H.S., C.P. Ewing, A.F. O'Connell, Jr., E.M. Bosler, J.G. Daley & M.W. Sayre. 1991. Increased population densities of *Amblyomma americanum* (Acari: Ixodidae) on Long Island, New York. *J. Parasitol.* **77**:493-495.

Ginsberg, H.S., K. E. Hyland, R. Hu, T.J. Daniels, & R.C. Falco. 1998. Tick population trends and forest type. *Science* **281**:349-350.

Ginsberg, H.S. and F.J. Rohlf. 1985. *Distribution and dispersal of mosquitoes, Fire Island National Seashore*. National Park Service, Office of Scientific Studies, Report No. **OSS 86-1**. 171 pp.

Ginsberg, H.S. & K.C. Stafford. Management of ticks and tick-borne diseases. *In* J. Goodman, D. Dennis, & D. Sonenshine (eds.) *Tickborne diseases of humans*. ASM Press, Washington, D.C. in press.

Ginsberg, H.S. & E. Zhioua. 1996. Nymphal survival and habitat distribution of *Ixodesm scapularis* and *Amblyomma americanum* ticks (Acari: Ixodidae) on Fire Island,New York, USA. *Exp. Appl. Acarol.* **20**:533-544.

Ginsberg, H.S. & E. Zhioua. 1999. Influence of deer abundance on abundance of questing adult *Ixodes scapularis* (Acari: Ixodidae). *J. Med. Entomol.* **36**:376-381.

Goddard, L.B., A.E. Roth, W.K. Reisen, et al. 2002. Vector competence of California mosquitoes for West Nile virus. *Emerging Infectious Diseases* **8**:1385-1391.

Goodman, R.A., E.C. Hawkins, N.J. Olby, C.B. Grindem, B. Hegarty, & E.B.Breitschwerdt. 2003. Molecular identification of *Ehrlichia ewingii* infection in dogs: 15 cases (1997-2001*). J. Am. Vet. Med. Assoc.* **222**:1102-1107.

Guirgis, S.S. & J.F. Sanzone. 1978. New records of mosquitoes in Suffolk County,Long Island, New York. *Mosq. News* **38**:200-203.

Grimstad, P.R. 1988. California group virus disease. pp. 99-136 *In* T.P. Monath (ed.) *The arboviruses: epidemiology and ecology*, vol. II. CRC Press, Boca Raton, FL.

Hanrahan, J.P., J.L. Benach, J.L. Coleman, E.M. Bosler, D.L. Morse, D.J. Cameron, R.Edelman, and R.A. Kaslow. 1984. Incidence and cumulative frequency of Lymedisease in an endemic community. *J. Infect. Dis.* **50**:489-496.

Harwood, R.F. & M.T. James. 1979. *Entomology in human and animal health*, 7th edition. Macmillan, NY.

Hayes, E.B. and M.E. Schriefer. 2002. Vaccination against Lyme biorreliosis. pp. 281- 300. *In* J.S. Gray, O. Kahl, R.S. Lane, and G. Stanek (eds*.) Lyme borreliosis, biology, epidemiology and control.* Wallingford, UK, CABI Publishing, 347 pp.

James, A,M., D. Liveris, G.P. Wormser, I. Schwartz, M.A. Montecalvo, and B.J. Johnson. 2001. *Borrelia lonestari* infection after a bite by an *Amblyomma americanum* tick. *J. Infect. Dis.* **183**:1810-1814.

Jamnbach, H., E. Berg, & E. Whitney. 1965. A review of arbovirus surveillance in Long Island, 1959-1963. *Proc. NJ Mosq. Exterm. Assoc.* **52**:166-174.

Kierans, J.E. & T.R. Litwak. 1989. Pictorial key to the adults of hard ticks, family Ixodidae (Ixodida: Ixodoidea), east of the Mississippi River. *J. Med. Entomol.* **26**:435-448.

Komar, N. 2000. West Nile viral encephalitis. *Rev. sci. tech. Off. int. Epiz.* 19:166-178.

Komar, N., S. Langevin, S. Hinten, N. Nemeth, E. Edwards, D. Hettler, et al. 2003. Experimental infection of North American birds with the New York 1999 strain of West Nile virus. *Emerging Infectious Diseases* **9**:311-322.

Kulasekera, V., L. Kramer, R.S. Nasci, et al. 2001. West Nile Virus infection in mosquitoes, birds, horses, and humans, Staten Island, New York, 2000. *Emerging* Infectious Diseases **7**:722-725.

Lanciotti R.S., J.T. Roehrig , V. Deubel, J. Smith, M. Parker, K. Steele, B. Crise, K.E. Volpe, M.B. Crabtree, J.H. Scherret, R.A. Hall, J.S. MacKenzie, C.B. Cropp, B. Panigrahy, E. Ostlund, B. Schmitt, M. Malkinson, C. Banet, J. Weissman J, N. Komar, H.M. Savage, W. Stone, T. McNamara, D.J. Gubler. 1999. Origin of the West Nile virus responsible for an outbreak of encephalitis in the northeastern United States. *Science* **286**:2333-2337.

Lane, R.S., J. Piesman, & W. Burgdorfer. 1991. Lyme borreliosis: relation of its causative agent to its vectors and hosts in North America and Europe. *Annual Review of Entomology* **36**:587-609.

LeDuc, J.W. 1987. Epidemiology and ecology of the California serogroup viruses. *Am. J. Trop. Med. Hyg.* **37(3 Suppl)**:60S-68S

Levin, M.L. & D. Fish. 2001. Interference between the agents of Lyme disease and human granulocytic ehrlichiosis in a natural reservoir host. *Vector Borne Zoon. Dis.* **1**:139-148.

Lussier, C. M. 2003. *Distribution and comparative trapping of mosquitoes in NPS units in the Northeastern United States.* Master's Thesis, University of Rhode Island. Kingston, RI.

Martens, P & L. Hall. 2000. Malaria on the move: human population movement and malaria transmission. *Emerg. Inf. Dis.* **6**:103-109.

Maurin, M., J.S. Bakken, & J.S. Dummler. 2003. Antibiotic susceptibilities of *Anaplasma* (*Ehrlichia*) *phgocytophilum* strains from various geographic areas in the United States. *Antimicrob. Agents Chemother.* **47**:413-415.

McQuiston, J.H. & J.E. Childs. 2002. Q fever in humans and animals in the United States. *Vector Borne Zoonotic Dis.* **2**:179-191.

Means, R.G. 1979. Mosquitoes of New York. Part I. The genus *Aedes* Meigen. New York State Museum, Bull. No. 430a. 221 pp.

Means, R.G. 1987. Mosquitoes of New York. Part II. Genera of Culicidae other than *Aedes* occurring in New York. New York State Museum, Bull. No. 430b. 180 pp.

McCormick, J. 1975. *Environmental inventory of the Fire Island National Seashore and the William Floyd Estate, Suffolk County, New York.* Jack McCormick Associates, Inc., Devon, PA

McGowan, J.E., Jr., J.A. Bryam, & M.B. Gregg. 1973. Surveillance of arboviral encephalitis in the United States, 1955-1971. *Am. J. Epidemiol.* **97**:199-207.

Mixson, T.R., H.S. Ginsberg, S.R. Campbell, J.W. Sumner, & C.D. Paddock. 2004. Detection of *Ehrlichia chaffeensis* in adult and nymphal *Amblyomma americanum* (Acari: Ixodidae) ticks from Long Island, New York. J. Med. Entomol. **41**:1104-1110.

Morris, C.D. 1988. Eastern equine encephalomyelitis. pp. 1-20 *In* T.P. Monath (ed.) *The arboviruses: epidemiology and ecology*, vol. III. CRC Press, Boca Raton, FL.

Morris, C.D., E. Whitney, T.F. Bast, & R. Deibel. 1973. An outbreak of eastern equine encephalomyelitis in upstate New York during 1971. *Am. J. Trop. Med. Hyg.* **22:**561-566.

Mullen, G.& L. Durden (eds.) 2002. *Medical and Veterinary Entomology.* Academic Press. Amsterdam. 597 pp.

Northup, J.G. 1985. A progress report on the ecological inventory project, Fire Island National Seashore. National Park Service, North Atlantic region, Boston, MA.

Paddock, C.D. & J.E. Childs. 2003. *Ehrlichia chaffeensis*: a prototypical emerging pathogen. *Clin. Microbiol. Rev.* **16:**37-64.

Pancholi, P, C.P. Kolbert, P.D. Mitchell, K.D. Reed, Jr., J.S. Dumler, J.S. Bakken, S.R. Telford, 3rd, D.H. Persing. 1995. *Ixodes dammini* as a potential vector of human granulocytic ehrlichiosis. *J. Infect. Dis.* **172:**1007-1012.

Piesman, J. 2002. Ecology of *Borrelia burgdorferi* sensu lato in North America. pp. 223-249 In J.S. Gray, O. Kahl, R.S. Lane, & G. Stanek (eds.) *Lyme Borreliosis, Biology, Epidemiology and Control.* CABI Publishing. Oxon, UK.

Sardelis, M.R., M.J. Turell, D.J. Dohm, and M.L. O'Guinn. 2001. Vector competence of selected North American *Culex* and *Coquillettidia* mosquitoes for West Nile virus. *Emerging Infectious Diseases.* **7:**1-11.

Schulze, T.L., G.S. Bowen, E.M. Bosler, M.F. Lakat, W.E. Parkin, R. Altman, B.G. Ormiston, and J.K. Schisler. 1984. *Amblyomma americanum*: a potential vector of Lyme disease in New Jersey. *Science* **224:**601-603.

Scoles, G.A., M. Papero, L. Beati, and D. Fish. 2001. A relapsing fever group spirochete transmitted by *Ixodes scapularis* ticks. *Vector Borne Zoon. Dis.* **1:**21-34.

Service, M.W. 1993. *Mosquito Ecology, Field Sampling Methods*, 2nd ed. Elsevier Applied Sci4ence. London. 988 pp.

Sonenshine, D.E. 1991. *Biology of Ticks*, vol. 1. Oxford University Press, NY. 447 pp.

Sonenshine, D.E. 1993. *Biology of Ticks*, vol. 2. Oxford University Press, NY. 465 pp.

Sonenshine, D.E., R.S. Lane, & W.L. Nicholson. 2002. Ticks (Ixodida). pp. 517-558. *In* G. Mullen & L. Durden (eds.) *Medical and Veterinary Entomology.* Academic Press. Amsterdam.

Spielman, A. 1976. Human babesiosis on Nantucket Island. Transmission by nymphal *Ixodes* ticks. *Am. J. Trop. Med. Hyg.* **25:**784-787.

Spielman, A., C.M. Clifford, J. Piesman, & M.D. Corwin. 1979. Human babesiosis on Nantucket Island, USA: description of the vector, *Ixodes* (*Ixodes*) *dammini* n. sp.(Acarina: Ixodidae). *J. Med. Entomol.* **15:**218-234.

Spielman, A., M.L. Wilson, J.F. Levine, & J. Piesman. 1985. Ecology of *Ixodes dammini*-borne babesiosis and Lyme disease. *Ann. Rev. Entomol.* **30:**439-460.

Srihongse, S., J.P. Woodall, M.A. Grayson, R. Deibel, T.F. Bast, C.D. Morris, E.M. Bosler, J.L. Benach, J.J. Howard, & J. Berlin. 1980. Arboviruses in New York State: surveillance in arthropods and nonhuman vertebrates, 1972-1977. *Mosq. News* **40:**269-276.

Stafford, K.C. and U. Kitron. 2002. Environmental management for Lyme borreliosis control. pp. 301-334. *In* J.S. Gray, O. Kahl, R.S. Lane, and G. Stanek (eds.*) Lyme Borreliosis, Biology, Epidemiology and Control.* CABI Publishing, Oxon, UK.

Telford, S.R., 3rd, P.M. Armstrong, P. Katavolos, I. Foppa, A.S. Olmeda Garcia, M.L. Wilson, & A. Spielman. 1997. A new Tick-Borne Encephalitis-like virus infecting New England deer ticks, *Ixodes dammini. Emerg. Infect. Dis.* **3:**165-170.

Tsai, T.F. & C.J. Mitchell. 1989. St. Louis Encephalitis. pp. 113-143 *In* T.P. Monath (ed.*) The arboviruses: epidemiology and ecology*, vol. IV. CRC Press, Boca Raton, FL.

Tsai, T.F. & T.P. Monath. 1987. Viral diseases in North America transmitted by arthropods or from vertebrate reservoirs. pp. 1417-1456 *In* R.D. Feigin & J.D. Cherry (eds.) *Textbook of pediatric infectious diseases*, vol. II, 2nd ed. Saunders, Philadelphia.

Turrell, M.J., M.L. O'Guinn, D.J. Dohm, et al. 2001. Vector competence of North American mosquitoes (Diptera: Culicidae) for West Nile Virus. *Journal of Medical Entomology* **38:**130-134.

Underwood, H.B., F.D. Verret, & J.P. Fischer. 1998. *Density and herd composition of white-tailed deer populations on Fire Island National Seashore.* Final Report to the National Park Service, New England System Support office, Boston, MA.

Vianna, N.J. & A.R. Hinman. 1971. Rocky Mountain spotted fever on Long Island. Epidemiologic and clinical aspects. *Am. J. Med.* **51:**725-730.

Wallace, B.J., G. Brady, D.M. Ackman, S.J. Wong, G. Jacquette, E.E. Lloyd, & G.S. Birkhead. 1998. Human granulocytic ehrlichiosis in New York. *Arch. Intern. Med.* **158:**769-773.

Wallis, R.C., R.M. Taylor, & J.R. Henderson. 1960. Isolation of Eastern Encephalomyelitis virus from *Aedes vexans* in Connecticut. *Proc. Soc. Exp. Biol. & Med.* **103:**442-444.

Wernsdorfer, W.H. & I. McGregor. 1988. *Malaria: principles and practices of malariology.* Churchill Livingstone, Edinburgh, New York.

White D.J., H.G. Chang, J.L. Benach, E.M. Bosler, S.C. Meldrum, R.G. Means, J.G. Debbie, G.S. Birkhead, & D.L. Morse. 1991. The geographic spread and temporal increase of the Lyme disease epidemic. *JAMA* **266:**1269-1270.

White, D.J. & M.K. Flynn. 1990. Rocky Mountain spotted fever in New York State. *Ann. NY Acad. Sci.* **590:**248-255.

Wilson, M.L. and R.D. Deblinger. 1993. Vector management to reduce the risk of Lyme disease. pp. 126-156. *In* H.S. Ginsberg (ed.) *Ecology and environmental management of Lyme disease.* New Brunswick, NJ, Rutgers University Press. 224 pp.

Zaki, M.H. 1979. Arthropod-borne viral encephalitides, illusion or reality in Suffolk County. *NY State J. Med.* **May 1979:**902-903.

Zhioua, E., H.S. Ginsberg, R.A. Humber, & R.A. LeBrun. 1999. Preliminary survey for entomopathogenic fungi associated with *Ixodes scapularis* (Acari: Ixodidae) in southern New York and New England, USA. *J. Med. Entomol.* **36:**635-637.

APPENDIX 1

2003 Mosquito Surveillance and Management Protocol Fire Island National Seashore

The purpose of this plan is to present a surveillance protocol to monitor mosquito populations from Fire Island National Seashore and to test mosquitoes for evidence of arboviral infection. Surveillance efforts focus on possible mosquito infection with Eastern Equine Encephalitis virus (EEE) and West Nile Virus (WNV). **Fire Island National Seashore will carry out a sanitation program to reduce artificial *Culex* larval habitat on lands administered by the national seashore, and will institute this surveillance and management protocol to minimize any risk of viral transmission.** The plan outlines appropriate additional actions if data indicate increasing risk of mosquito-borne disease.

In light of continued uncertainty over how West Nile Virus and other mosquito-borne diseases will manifest themselves in the Western Hemisphere this year, proactive management is again proposed for 2003 and will follow very similar protocols to those used in the last four years. These guidelines will continue to be reexamined in subsequent years, based on increased knowledge of and experience with arboviruses in this area. The need for responses based on unpredictable trends in the spread of viruses requires that a consultation process be established that will allow appropriate responses to changes in mosquito populations and viral infection patterns as they occur. This consultation will include NPS, other DOI, CDC, NY State, Suffolk County, and/or local experts. The consultation process can range from communication between park staff and local, state, or federal experts via telephone, FAX, or e-mail, to scheduled meetings and site visits, depending on the degree of risk of local viral transmission.

Criteria for active management within the park:

Presence of WNV in or near the park, or of EEE in the park, or extraordinarily persistent and/or high levels of EEE infection in mosquitoes near the park, could trigger interventions within the park if conditions are such that:

1) the conditions strongly suggest disease risk to humans;
2) the risk of disease transmission would be substantially lowered by the intervention; and
3) mosquito management within the park is superior to other available approaches to manage disease risk.

The decision to apply mosquito management interventions will depend on the intensity and persistence of viral activity, proximity of viral activity to mosquito emergence sites within Fire Island National Seashore, time of year, mosquito population levels, etc. Because these conditions vary from year to year, and cannot be predicted, this consultation process will be used to determine whether interventions within the park are warranted, on a case by case basis.

Interventions can include closing portions of the park to the public, mosquito management methods such as applications of *Bacillus thuringiensis israelensis* (*Bti*) or *Bacillus sphaericus* (*Bs*) to prevent emergences, or adulticide applications to areas with high levels of adult *Culex* spp.or *Aedes (formerly Aedes) sollicitans*. The final decision on all management interventions within Fire Island National Seashore, including the William Floyd Estate, will be made by the Park Superintendent in accordance with NPS Management Policies.

Specific criteria for level of surveillance and management:

Three levels of action are proposed: (1) Surveillance and Education, (2) Detection and Public Notification, and (3) Mosquito Management. Based on monitoring data, guidelines are presented for deciding what criteria would result in a move to the next higher level of surveillance and management. Arrangements to send mosquitoes for viral testing should be completed by the end of June at the latest. Similarly, arrangements for pesticide applications or other management interventions (to be applied if necessary, according to this protocol) should be completed by the end of June. These arrangements will include permit approval, arranging for applicators, etc. Decisions to move to higher levels will be made by park staff, in consultation with appropriate experts.

Level (1) - Surveillance and Education

Education consists of park brochures, interpretive programs, etc., to inform the public about mosquitoes, their roles in natural systems, potential disease transmission, and associated surveillance and management programs. Basic surveillance consists of passive surveillance for dead birds, and mosquito monitoring including larval monitoring with pint dippers and adult monitoring using CDC miniature light traps baited with carbon dioxide, and gravid traps.

The gravid traps are intended to sample gravid *Culex* spp., and to be sensitive indicators of the presence of WNV. The CDC traps are intended to sample host-seeking female mosquitoes of several species (including *Aedes sollicitans* and *Culex* spp.) to provide broader surveillance of viral infection in potentially human-biting mosquitoes. Therefore, gravid traps will be placed in or near potential *Culex* larval habitat, and CDC traps will be placed at sites where mosquitoes are likely to encounter humans, or between mosquito breeding sites and potential human-encounter sites. Guidance for trap placement will be obtained from the report "Distribution and dispersal of mosquitoes, Fire Island National Seashore" (H.S. Ginsberg & F.J. Rohlf. 1985. Report #OSS-86-1, National Park Service, Boston, MA) and by consultation with mosquito biologists.

One gravid trap will be placed near the freshwater wetlands in the secondary dune area at Hospital Point, and one CDC trap will be placed in the woods in the Smith Shores area between the Hospital Point marsh and the Smith Point Ranger Station. At the William Floyd Estate (WFE), one gravid trap will be placed in moist woodland habitat and one gravid trap will be placed near the salt marsh/woods border. Additional traps may be placed at any freshwater swamp sites that have potential for *Culiseta melanura* breeding.

Additional traps will be set at other sites along Fire Island, as follows:

One gravid trap will be placed near the Watch Hill/Davis Park border and another placed near the park houses at Watch Hill. One CDC trap will be placed at Sailors Haven, one gravid trap will be placed in the Sunken Forest, and one gravid trap will be placed in or near wetlands in the Lighthouse tract.

This initial distribution of traps may be modified based on surveillance results. For example, if there are positive results in birds or mosquitoes in an area, additional traps can be added to this area to get more complete information about the local epizootiology of the virus.

Traps will be set once each week, June – September (traps at different sites may be placed on different nights, to facilitate timely setting and collecting of traps). Trap catches will be sorted to species, and the number of *Culex* spp., *Aedes sollicitans* -- and other mosquito species as time permits -- will be counted. During large emergences, trap counts and species composition will be estimated using appropriate techniques.

Virus testing: mosquitoes captured in the surveillance traps will be sorted to species and placed in pools using appropriate techniques. A pool will consist of up to 50 mosquitoes of a single species from a single trap (pool size is recommended by testing lab). Pools of *Culex* spp. and *Aedes sollicitans* will be sent to the laboratory for detection of WNV and EEE virus by cell culture, or other technique approved by Park staff. Pools of other species can also be sent for viral testing, at the discretion of Park staff.

Larval monitoring: mosquito larvae will be monitored using a pint dipper. Sampling sites will be selected by reference to Ginsberg & Rohlf (1985) and/or by consultation with mosquito biologists, and modified by current experience. At least 25 dips will be taken at each site, the larvae counted, and representative specimens returned to the lab to confirm identifications (see Ginsberg & Rohlf 1985), as time permits. Larvae will be sampled at sites near the gravid traps at least once per month in the absence of WNV. Should virus be found in the seashore, larvae will be sampled as often as recommended by mosquito experts.

Dead birds: passive monitoring for dead birds will include alerting park rangers, interpreters, and resource management staff to be on the lookout for dead birds. Reports of bird mortality will be investigated by resource management staff, and candidates for possible viral infection will be collected and submitted for testing using a protocol developed by the park in accordance with guidelines from the U.S. Fish and Wildlife Service, the Centers for Disease Control, New York State and the Suffolk County Health Department.

Criteria for move to Level (2):

Substantial mosquito trap catches will result in a move to Level (2). The term "substantial" is defined as a catch of over 1,000 female mosquitoes in a carbon dioxide-baited CDC light trap from Fire Island, or of over 100 individuals in a trap on the William Floyd Estate. Also, detection of WNV or EEE virus in birds, mammals, or mammal-feeding mosquitoes on Fire

Island or at mainland Long Island sites within five miles of Fire Island or of the William Floyd Estate will trigger an increase to Level (2) surveillance. Detection of EEE virus in bird-feeding mosquitoes (e.g., *Cs. melanura*) will trigger a move to Level (2) if there are signs of higher than normal prevalence (e.g., at least three pools of *Cs. melanura* positive for EEE within five miles of Smith Point or of the William Floyd Estate).

Level (2) - Detection and Public Notification

The park will notify Suffolk County Vector Control of the results of the surveillance program. If WNV or EEE is detected within the park, visitors to the park will also be notified about mosquito densities, possibility of viral infection (realistic assessment), and self-protection methods they can use to minimize the number of mosquito bites. Arrangements will be finalized for pesticide application in case conditions warrant such intervention (this should be coordinated with Suffolk County Vector Control). Consultation will be initiated between Fire Island National Seashore and Suffolk County Vector Control, New York State Health Department, Centers for Disease Control, U.S. Department of the Interior, and/or experts from universities or other institutions to guide the Park Superintendent on potential courses of action. Larval management in artificial sites will be intensified and surveillance will continue.

Criteria for move to Level (3):

Detection of WNV in a potential human biter (e.g., *Culex salinarius* or *Ae. sollicitans*), or of EEE in a potential epidemic vector (e.g., *Ae. sollicitans, Coquillettidia perturbans, Aedes vexans*) in the park will trigger the consultation process to assess the risk of disease transmission. In general, single positive mosquito pools will result in intensified surveillance (increased trapping and larval sampling), and multiple positive pools will result in an increase to level (3). Signs of increasing WNV epizootic activity (e.g., positive birds followed by positive mosquito pools, or multiple and increasing numbers of positive birds over a two-week period) can result in an increase to level (3), based on the consultation process. Detection of WNV or EEE in potential epidemic vectors outside but near the park, persistent high levels of EEE in *Cs. melanura* at sites within 5 miles of the park (at least three EEE isolations at a site in consecutive samples taken within one month) at the same time as evidence of an imminent emergence of *Ae. sollicitans*, or other evidence of EEE activity (e.g., animal cases) within 5 miles of the park will trigger the consultation process to assess the risk of disease transmission. The consultation can result in an increase to Level (3) if such action is deemed appropriate by the Park Superintendent after consultation with the appropriate experts and in accordance with NPS Management Policies.

Level (3) - Mosquito Management

The approach to mosquito management will depend on the nature of the disease risk, as projected from the surveillance data. Detection of EEE activity by PCR or ELISA is not, by itself, sufficient evidence of EEE activity to trigger mosquito management within the park. EEE activity must be detected by cell culture, or by other suitably rigorous technique approved by park staff, before mosquito management is initiated in the park. Detection methods for WNV will be based on Centers for Disease Control (CDC) recommendations and approved by park staff.

(3a)   Epidemic vector infected with EEE in Fire Island National Seashore

    i.   EEE detected in *Ae. sollicitans* (or other potential epidemic vector) on Fire Island.

Intervention: Application of adulticide (resmethrin, permethrin, or other material approved by park staff) to Fire Island, if appropriate according to consultation process. Pesticide will be applied to the site of viral identification and to the barrier island for distances in both directions from the identification site(s) determined by the consultation process, and stopping at appropriate natural borders. Multiple viral isolations can result in more extensive adulticide application, determined by the consultation process, based on specifics of viral spread. Similarly, single isolations at remote sites can result in less extensive, finely-targeted application(s). Larviciding can occur in natural areas with high larval densities of potential vector species.

    ii.   EEE detected in *Ae. sollicitans* (or other potential epidemic vector) at the William Floyd Estate.

  Intervention: Application of adulticide to the William Floyd Estate, if appropriate according to consultation process.

    iii.   Potential human vector mosquito species positive for WNV in an area with previously-demonstrated epizootic activity (previous positive mosquito pools or multiple positive vertebrates)

Intervention: Based on consultation process. A single mosquito pool positive for WNV would typically result in increased trapping to assess risk of human disease. Multiple positive pools in an area with previously-demonstrated epizootic activity could result in adulticide and/or larvicide application, as in (3a) section i.

(3b) Multiple WNV or EEE detections in vertebrate(s) in Fire Island National Seashore

Intervention: Based on consultation process. Interventions can include increased mosquito trapping and testing, and increased larval management and/or adulticiding when there is evidence of intensive epizootic activity (e.g., numerous or increasing numbers of positive birds within a two-week period, or positive birds coupled with positive mosquito pools), especially when accompanied by high mosquito numbers (e.g., *Culex* in carbon dioxide-baited CDC trap catch >

31

500 females/trap; *Ae. sollicitans* in carbon dioxide-baited CDC trap catch > 2,500 females/trap).

(3c)   WNV or EEE detected outside but near the park, or in enzootic vectors within the park, with current or imminent emergence of epidemic vector species within the park.

i.   WNV: Multiple evidence of WNV in mosquitoes or vertebrates within two miles of Fire Island National Seashore can trigger adulticide application within the park if populations of *Culex* spp. are high (trap catches >500 females in carbon dioxide baited CDC light trap on Fire Island, >50 females in CDC trap at WFE) or of *Ae. sollicitans* are high (trap catches >2,500 females in CDC trap on Fire Island, >250 females in CDC trap at WFE) in park areas within two miles of the viral isolations. Location and extent of application will be based on consultation process. Response at lower adult densities, especially with evidence of imminent emergence from larval samples, will be based on the consultation process, and can include larval management.

ii.   EEE: Evidence of EEE within 5 miles of Fire Island National Seashore, or in *Cs. melanura* within the park, will trigger the consultation process. Park staff will contact the CDC (initially by phone, FAX, or e-mail, with more comprehensive consultation only if necessary), NY State, Suffolk County, U.S. Department of Interior, university, and/or other experts as needed. If conditions warrant (according to the CDC and in consultation with other appropriate experts, to lower the risk of human disease) appropriate interventions can be applied in accordance with NPS Management Policies.

Howard S. Ginsberg, Ph.D.
USGS Patuxent Wildlife Research Center
2003

APPENDIX 2

2003 Mosquito Action Plan (Map) Fire Island National Seashore (8/12/03)

Reviewed By _____   Date _____
                            (Deputy Superintendent)

Approved By _____   Date _____
                            (Superintendent)

Introduction

Fire Island is a 32-mile long barrier beach approximately 1-5 miles south of Long Island. Fire Island National Seashore (FIIS) is located in the middle 26 miles of the island. The park has concurrent jurisdiction with New York State that encompasses 1,000 feet into the Atlantic Ocean and 4,000 feet into the Great South Bay including the islands adjacent to the bay shoreline. There are 17 communities within the boundaries of the park, 13 of which are within the West District. There are approximately 4,100 homes on Fire Island all within the park's boundary, including two incorporated villages, which have their own governing bodies. Of the 4,100 homes, approximately 350-500 of the residences are year round. Visitation on a peak season weekend day can be as high as 100,000 within the park areas and the communities combined.

Fire Island National Seashore has the responsibility to preserve the park natural resources. It is a responsibility of the park to monitor park mosquito populations, manage park natural processes, and assist in the protection of visitor and resident health. In 1985, based on research on mosquito dispersal, the park determined that the impact of mosquitoes in the federal wilderness area was minimal on nearby Long Island south shore communities.

In the late 1990's public concern relating to Eastern Equine Encephalitis and West Nile Virus, both diseases related to mosquito populations, prompted the park to initiate mosquito monitoring. To further limit the possibility of a major incident and to ensure a quick and rational response should a mosquito-borne disease be found in this area, the park has developed the following Mosquito Action Plan (MAP).

Fire Island National Seashore West Nile Virus Action Plan

Pre-Season Preparations

During this stage the park receives low to moderate visitation and mosquito activity is dormant to low. The primary goal of this stage is to prepare for the season ahead.

1. All Stage Three Incident (see below) Caches should be checked to ensure that personal protective equipment (PPE) is maintained or replaced from the previous year. Those employees that are incidental responders in the field will have access to Tyvek tick suits, head nets, gloves and insect repellant at each ranger station in the park (William Floyd Estate, Smith Point, Watch Hill, Sailor's Haven, Lighthouse). These items are stored in locked, weather-resistant caches at each station. Caches will be checked and restocked as necessary. See Appendix D for equipment cache information.

2. All dead bird transport coolers (see below) should be checked to ensure that the equipment and protocols are maintained and current. Each ranger station in the park has a cooler with PPE and other items needed to collect and transport dead birds in accordance with state and federal guidelines.

3. Park employees should be informed of the preparations underway and educated about disease prevention including sanitation and personal protection. The education program in the park should be started at the first staff meeting of the New Year (just to remind everyone of what is on the way). Employees should know how the disease is transmitted, how to prevent breeding areas from forming around the workplace or at home, and how to protect themselves. All employees should also be taught to recognize the signs and symptoms of West Nile Virus (see appendix A).

4. All park areas should be checked to identify any potential artificial freshwater mosquito breeding areas. Work orders should be generated to clean up these areas. This should include evaluating park vehicle access roads (Burma Road, road to facilities, etc.). Those areas that have significant rutting that retain standing water longer then 2-3 days may need to be graded or filled. Sanitation actions should continue until October, when mosquito breeding activity ceases (see Appendix E).

5. Park Management Protocols, educational/outreach documents (mosquito brochure, interpretive programs), and other brochures and handouts should be prepared and management plans finalized. Education should consist of brochures, interpretive programs, press releases or other means to inform the public.

6. Permit approvals for pesticide applications or other management interventions should be obtained and should include all possible regulated chemicals for mosquito management use. This is done in partnership with Suffolk County Vector Control. Permit applications are made to the National Park Service Integrated Pest Management coordinator for FIIS.

7. The Mosquito Action Plan (MAP) should be prepared in accordance with the Mosquito Surveillance and Management Protocol. This plan should include a protocol for handling dead birds and should be reviewed and approved by the MAP committee.

8. Adult mosquito trapping sites and larval sampling sites should be chosen in consultation with park experts and scientists at the United States Geological Survey – Biological Research Division.

9. Arrangements should be made with Suffolk County Vector Control or other agencies for transport and testing of mosquitoes, dead birds, etc.

Stage One – Active Surveillance And Education

This stage begins in the summer when park visitation becomes moderate to high and mosquito activity is moderate to very high. The park will begin trapping mosquitoes and preparing pools of mosquitoes to be tested, in accordance with guidelines provided by the park's Mosquito Surveillance and Management Protocol. This will entail close work with Suffolk County Vector Control.

1. Education efforts by the park should be fully implemented. Interpretive programs, radio announcements and press releases should be used to educate staff and the general public. Park

brochures, handouts, and other sources of information should be distributed to all the visitor centers and, where appropriate and workable, in Fire Island communities. Employees should be sufficiently knowledgeable to provide residents and visitors with accurate information (or know where they can get it). However, it is critical that all employees realize that the Superintendent or his/her designee is the only one speaking to the media for the park.

2. The protocol for handling dead birds should be distributed and promoted. Fire Island employees, residents and visitors should understand what to do if they find a dead bird.

3. Mosquitoes will be collected once a week from each of nine traps set out at the William Floyd Estate and from Smith Point to the Lighthouse. These mosquitoes will be transported live back to PMF, where they will be sorted into the main vector species and stored on dry ice until delivered to Suffolk County Vector Control as soon as practicable but before Friday noon.

4. Dead birds will be collected in accordance with the park's protocol (see Appendix B).

Stage Two – Detection And Public Notification

This stage occurs when routine mosquito monitoring indicates a potential emergence of adult mosquitoes, or West Nile Virus or Eastern Equine Encephalitis has been detected in or within 2 miles of the park. Visitation is probably high and mosquito activity high to very high. The park will notify Suffolk County of a potential emergence. If disease is detected in or near the park, visitors will be notified, informed of the (realistic) potential for contracting disease and advised to use protection.

1. Field responders should be reminded of the resources available to them (equipment caches etc.)

2. In the event that disease is detected, education efforts by the park should be intensified. More frequent interpretive talks, community outreach and active distribution of brochures or handouts by rangers are a few ways to do this. Press releases should be generated (see Appendix C).

3. In the event that disease is detected, the park will consult with the Centers for Disease Control (CDC), Suffolk County Vector Control, New York State Health Department, New York State Department of Environmental Conservation and other authorities. Together with these agencies, the park will decide on the best course of action to minimize the risk to human health, and determine the possible environmental impact of any action taken.

4. In the event that disease is detected, arrangements for pesticide use should be finalized. The park should work closely with Suffolk County Vector Control and any other involved parties to assure that, should the need arise, application of pesticides is done within the guidelines approved by NPS, CDC, EPA and DEC.

Stage Three – Mosquito Management

This stage will be triggered by the detection of disease in more than one group ("pool") of mosquitoes or by detection of disease in both mosquitoes and birds, or in increasing numbers of birds. Mosquito management could take several forms: application of adulticide to the identification site, application of larvicide to breeding areas, and/or closing areas of the park to the public.

1. All of the actions listed above for Stage Two should be immediately implemented, if not already done.

2. The park's response will conform to the Suffolk County Unified Command (SCUC) structure and the NPS Incident Command System (ICS). Park headquarters will be the Command Center, with supply, public relations and administration functions.

3. The Superintendent/Incident Commander will close areas of the park as needed or appropriate. This may impact large areas of the park such as a marina or the William Floyd Estate, or just specific trails.

4. There should be a daily radio brief to the staff as part of the incident command process. Public information efforts should be coordinated with the CDC and SCUC to prevent duplication of work and assure that information is consistent.

Post-Incident Stage

This stage is the evaluation period to immediately follow a Stage Three incident.

1. If Stage Three was reached, each response team leader, district ranger or other supervisor should hold discussions with his/her staff and be prepared to make a presentation to the Incident Commander and overhead no later that one pay period after the Stage Three incident has concluded. The Incident Commander and overhead team should be prepared to hold a supervisor's critique based on the above time line.

2. The superintendent will schedule an all-employee staff meeting no later than two pay periods after the Incident Commander concludes his/her critique.

3. The park management team should quickly evaluate current conditions and a return to the appropriate stage should begin immediately.

Post- Season Wrap-Up

At this point visitation is low and mosquito activity is low to dormant. The main purpose of this stage is to evaluate the past season and clean and store all equipment.

1. A final report will be written, detailing the results of the season's mosquito surveillance and management activities.

2. All monitoring equipment will be cleaned and put into safe storage.

Prepared by the FIIS Mosquito Action Plan Committee (in alphabetical order):
James Ebert, William Flanagan, Steve Henderson, Marie Lawrence, Jay Lippert, Richard Stavdal.

Appendix A (of the 2003 Mosquito Action Plan)

Questions and answers on West Nile virus/encephalitis for employees and visitors of Fire Island National Seashore

What is West Nile Encephalitis?
"Encephalitis" means an inflammation of the brain and can be caused by bacteria and viruses, including viruses transmitted by mosquitoes. West Nile Encephalitis is an infection of the brain caused by West Nile Virus (WNV), a virus commonly found in Africa, West Asia, and the Middle East. West Nile Virus is also found in southern Europe. It was found in the Western Hemisphere for the first time in 1999. It is closely related to St. Louis Encephalitis virus, also found in the United States.

How big a threat is West Nile Virus to the health and safety of NPS employees and visitors?
Since its introduction into the Western Hemisphere, West Nile Virus has proven to be most serious in the elderly and people who are already weakened by other ailments. Since 1999, when the virus first appeared in the Northeast, it has spread westward. The Centers for Disease Control reports that in 2002, WNV occurred in 44 states with 284 fatalities. People most likely to develop serious symptoms are the elderly and those who are already ill. By using insect repellents when engaged in outside activities, the risk of contracting West Nile Virus can be greatly lowered. For maximum protection, a repellent containing 33% DEET is recommended. Follow the label directions carefully, especially when using DEET on children.

What is the basic transmission cycle for the West Nile virus?
Mosquitoes become infected when they feed on virus infected birds. After an incubation period infected mosquitoes can transmit West Nile virus to humans and or other animals. Disease symptoms do not develop in everyone that is bitten by an infected mosquito. Elderly and physically weak or ill people are more likely to develop symptoms.

How long has West Nile virus been in the United States?
It is not known how long the virus has been in the U.S., but the Centers for Disease Control and Prevention (CDC) scientists first detected it in the eastern U.S. during the summer of 1999.

How do people get West Nile Virus?
Transmission comes through the bite of a mosquito (primarily the *Culex spp.*) that is infected with the West Nile Virus. The virus is located in the mosquito's salivary glands. The virus is not known to be transmitted by casual contact between people, but in a small number of cases it has been transmitted by blood transfusions, organ transplants, breastfeeding and even during pregnancy from mother to baby.

What are the symptoms of West Nile Virus?
Most people who are infected with WNV have no symptoms. Some experience flu-like symptoms including fever, headache, and body aches, often with skin rash and swollen lymph

glands. In fewer cases, the infection may be more severe and may include headache, high fever, neck stiffness, stupor, disorientation, coma, tremors, convulsions, muscle weakness, paralysis. Severe infection may lead to permanent neurological damage or death in the most extreme cases.

What is the treatment for West Nile Virus?
There is no specific treatment for West Nile Virus. Mild cases usually clear up on their own. In more severe cases, intensive supportive therapy is indicated including hospitalization, IV fluids and nutrition, and good nursing care. If you develop symptoms of severe WNV illness, such as unusually severe headaches or confusion, seek medical attention immediately.

Is there a vaccine against West Nile Virus?
There is no vaccine for the West Nile Virus at this time.

Can a person get West Nile Encephalitis directly from birds that might have the virus?
There is evidence that a person with a cut can get West Nile Encephalitis from handling live or dead birds that test positive for the virus. To be safe, always use gloves or double plastic bags to handle or remove dead birds.

Is a woman's pregnancy at risk if she gets West Nile encephalitis?
There is evidence that an infection caused by the West Nile virus can be transmitted to the non-born child of a pregnant woman. The Centers for Disease Control recommends that pregnant women avoid being bitten (stay away from mosquitoes and use repellent).

Why doesn't Fire Island National Seashore spray for mosquitoes?
Fire Island National Seashore is by law required to protect the native wildlife, plants and other natural resources within its boundaries from environmental contamination. Modern insecticides, while safer for humans than their older counterparts, are often very toxic to fish and other forms of marine life.

Since 1999, Fire Island National Seashore, in cooperation with Suffolk County, and in consultation with New York State and the Centers for Disease Control, has conducted a mosquito surveillance program each summer to monitor mosquitoes on park lands for the presence of diseases that present a threat to humans, such as Eastern Equine Encephalitis and West Nile Virus. The program was designed by a leading entomologist from the University of Rhode Island.

Each week, mosquitoes are sent to Albany to be tested for disease. If mosquito-borne disease is found in the park, or within a few miles of park boundaries, the National Park Service will consult with the County, the CDC, New York State and with academic experts to decide whether or not to spray park lands to reduce the number of adult mosquitoes. Other control methods such as larviciding may also be implemented.

What role does the Centers for Disease Control and Prevention play in NPS mosquito management efforts?
The Centers for Disease Control and Prevention and other federal, state and local agencies will assist the National Park Service to determine the severity of the public health threat from

mosquito-borne disease in Fire Island National Seashore, and to choose the appropriate course of action to protect the health of staff, residents and visitors.

What can park visitors or park employees do to prevent becoming infected with the West Nile virus?
No control method will eliminate *all* mosquitoes. For the individual, the very best form of protection is personal protection. Avoid areas with mosquitoes, but if you must be outside, wear protective clothing and use repellent.

- Long-sleeved shirts, long pants, a hat, and gloves can provide increased protection from mosquitoes. For extra protection, clothing can also be treated with an insecticide such as permethrin.
- The use of an insect repellent on exposed skin will reduce your chances of being bitten by mosquitoes. A repellent with 20% to 30% DEET (N,N-diethyl-meta-toluamide) as the active ingredient works the best.
- The combination of permethrin-treated clothing and a DEET-based repellent on exposed skin will provide for maximum personal protection.
- The use of a head net and mesh jacket can also provide added protection and needed ventilation on warm days.

Where can I get more information on West Nile Virus and other mosquito borne diseases?
Check on the web at HYPERLINK http://www.cdc.gov/ncidod/dvbid/westnile/index.htm or call your local public health office.

Appendix B (of the 2003 Mosquito Action Plan)

2003 protocol for collecting dead birds on Fire Island National Seashore

The National Park Service, Fire Island National Seashore (NPS-FIIS) will work with the New York State Department of Environmental Conservation (DEC), Suffolk County Health Department and Suffolk County Vector Control (SCVC) to collect and transport bird carcasses. This will be done in accordance with guidelines developed by the U.S. Fish and Wildlife Service, the Centers for Disease Control, New York State and the Suffolk County Health Department.

For viral testing, the DEC definition of an acceptable bird carcass for collection and transportation is:

- The bird is a **crow**, a **raven**, a **blue jay** or a **raptor** (osprey, eagle, hawk, vulture, or falcon).
- The collector believes it **died within the past 18-24 hours** (the carcass is fresh, not bloated, infested or decayed).
- The collector believes **it did not die of routine natural causes or due to an accident**.

EVERY EFFORT SHOULD BE MADE TO COLLECT AND TRANSPORT CARCASSES TO THE PATCHOGUE MAINTENANCE FACILITY WITHIN A FEW HOURS SO THAT THE 24-HOUR PERIOD IS NOT PASSED.

List of dead-bird drop off locations on Fire Island National Seashore:

Lighthouse Annex (checkpoint)
Talisman
Sailors Haven
Watch Hill
Wilderness Visitor Center (Smith Point)

Rules for reporting, handling and transporting dead birds:

1. Safety first and foremost – **DO NOT TOUCH THE CARCASS WITH YOUR BARE HANDS!**

2. THE PERSON WHO FOUND THE BIRD (STAFF, RESIDENTS OR VISITORS) SHOULD **CALL THE SUFFOLK COUNTY DEAD BIRD HOTLINE IMMEDIATELY TO REPORT IT: (631) 853-8405.** Staff should explain to visitors that Suffolk County needs to assign a number to the specimen and to record time and date and a few details about the bird.

3. Suffolk County will then fax a report to FIIS staff headquarters (Fax # 631-289-4898) with the name and phone number of the person who found the bird. Whoever is on duty at KEC 700 (FIIS headquarters main desk) will then contact the FIIS dead-bird drop-off location (see

list above) nearest the person who found the bird so that arrangements can be made for a staff member to pick it up or for the person who found the bird to drop it off.

4. Whenever possible, carcass collection and handling should be done by those staff on the FIIS Dead Bird Collection List (see list below).

5. Collecting equipment will be found in the dead bird collection-and-transport coolers located at all ranger stations or visitor centers (Lighthouse Annex, Sailors Haven, Watch Hill, Smith Point –Wilderness Visitor Center, William Floyd Estate) and at Talisman. In the coolers will be large plastic bags, rubber gloves and specimen tags. THE TAGS ARE TO BE COMPLETED BY THE CARCASS COLLECTOR.

6. Collectors should wear rubber gloves (found in cooler).

7. The carcass is collected by inverting a plastic bag (found in cooler), grasping the bird, then pulling the bird into the bag.

8. The bag with the bird is sealed, then placed inside another plastic bag with a tag containing the following information:

- Where the bird was found
- Date and time the bird was found
- Collector's name
- Best estimate of what species it is (e.g. *Cyanocitta cristata*) and the common name (e.g. Blue Jay).

9. Place the bagged carcass in the dead bird transportation cooler with two or three blue ice packs (found in ranger/visitor station freezer). **DO NOT FREEZE THE BIRD.**

10. Remove the rubber gloves by turning one inside out, holding it with the other glove then turning that one inside out also. PLACE THE GLOVES IN THE COOLER.

11. Close the cooler securely and transport to the Patchogue Maintenance Facility (PMF) as quickly as possible by whatever means is available. At PMF there will be a large light gray dry ice cooler in the mosquito preparation area (near the bathroom). The cooler will be marked "DEAD BIRDS IN HERE." Place the bird in the cooler and close securely. The bird will be transported to SCVC with the next shipment of mosquitoes. The park has arranged with SCVC to keep dead birds on dry ice until delivered (dry ice will preserve the integrity of the virus, if any is present, but regular freezing will not).

12. Remove the used gloves from the transportation cooler and discard them into the box next to the sink marked "USED LATEX GLOVES." **Replace with a fresh pair** from the box of gloves on top of the sink. There will also be a box of plastic bags marked "for dead birds." **Replace the plastic bag you used** with a clean one from this box. **Return the dead bird cooler to the ranger station/visitor center it came from and make sure the blue ice packs go back into the freezer at the ranger station/visitor center.**

Below is a list of personnel recommended and authorized to remove dead birds for viral testing from the park:

Park Staff on Dead Bird Collection List (in alphabetical order):

Michael Bilecki	Marie Lawrence
Paul Czachor	April Lee
Steve Czarniecki	Jay Lippert
Jim Dunphy	Irene Rosen
Bernie Felix	Steve Singler
Steve Finn	Richard Stavdal
Steve Henderson	Mark Tripi
Joe Heinrich	Paula Valentine
Stacey Kopitsch	Wayne Valentine
Judy Lakomy	Mickey Walsh

Appendix C (of the 2003 Mosquito Action Plan)

DRAFT PRESS RELEASE

Date

West Nile Virus Found on Fire Island

Fire Island National Seashore Superintendent Dave Spirtes announced today that West Nile Virus-infected mosquitoes/birds have been found on Fire Island. The bird was found by _____ at _____. The mosquitoes were from a trap set by_____ (Suffolk County/the park as part of its weekly monitoring program). Testing was done by _____.

The National Park Service will be working closely with the Centers for Disease Control (CDC), the New York State Department of Environmental Conservation (DEC), Suffolk County Vector Control, and local Fire Island and Long Island municipalities to determine the best course of action to protect residents, visitors and employees of the Seashore. Actions to protect the public may include control methods such as larviciding or spraying. The public will be notified 24 hours in advance of any spray event.

The park is also conducting continued surveillance to monitor the severity and extent of West Nile Virus in the Seashore.

Residents, visitors and staff are advised to avoid mosquito-infested areas. If contact with mosquitoes is unavoidable, it is advisable to wear protective clothing and use an effective insect repellent, such as one containing at least 30% DEET. People most at risk of becoming ill from West Nile Virus are those over 50 years of age or whose health is impaired. Such people are advised to stay away from areas with mosquitoes.

For general information on West Nile Virus, please contact your local health department. Information can also be obtained from the CDC, New York State or Suffolk County WNV web sites, or one of the park visitor centers. If you have information or questions for the park, please contact our headquarters at (631) 289-4810.

Appendix D (of the 2003 Mosquito Action Plan)

Check List For Map Equipment Caches

Each ranger station at Fire Island National Seashore has Stage Three Personal Protective Equipment (PPE) stored in a clearly labeled black box. Each station also has a cooler for transporting dead birds. Boxes and coolers should be kept in an area with other protective equipment. They should be inspected periodically by District Rangers and the black PPE boxes should be kept locked. The key should be clearly marked and in an obvious, easily accessible location (such as a key box). Caches will be available to all staff involved in implementing MAP protocols. Caches are available at:

West District Ranger Station - Full cache
Sailors Haven Ranger Station/Shop - Full cache
Talisman Shop - Half cache
Watch Hill Ranger Station/Shop- Full cache
Wilderness Visitor Center- Half cache
William Floyd Estate- Half cache
Patchogue Maintenance Facility- Full cache

The following is the list of items in a full cache:

Stage Three PPE Black Box:

- 8 hoop style head nets
- 8 net style bug jackets
- 12 pr. Gloves
- 12 paper suits
- 1 case of repellant (4 cans)
- 4 "After Bite" pens
- one copy of the Mosquito Action Plan

Dead Bird Coolers:

- 12 large plastic bags
- six pairs of rubber gloves
- 6 - 12 bird carcass identification tags
- three blue plastic ice packs (to be placed in site area freezer from July 1 through September 15)

Additional PPE equipment is stored in black boxes at PMF in the Resource Management storage area (C4 key), in the building directly west of the main building.

Appendix E (of the 2003 Mosquito Action Plan)

Reduction Of Artificial Freshwater Mosquito Breeding Habitat On Park Lands

As stated in the Mosquito Surveillance and Management Protocol, Fire Island National Seashore will conduct a sanitation program to remove or reduce artificial larval habitat for the West Nile Virus vector, *Culex spp*. Such habitat is characterized by the presence of stagnant, dirty, fresh water. Fresh water that is present and undisturbed for 4 days or more and that contains a moderate to large quantity of organic matter (decaying vegetation; animal droppings; garbage of any kind; pollution or runoff from gardens, livestock holding pens, or other sources) is prime habitat for *Culex*. Following are suggestions from state and federal agencies in NY, NJ and elsewhere for where to look for *Culex* larval habitat and mechanical remedies to reduce the attractiveness of these areas to mosquitoes.

Underground Septic Tanks

Mosquitoes can enter through covers that don't fit properly, through cracks in the ground, or through vent pipes, and produce offspring in large numbers. Covers should be altered so that they fit adequately, cracks should be filled, and all vents should be covered with screening, preferably aluminum, to prevent the entry of females ready to lay eggs.

Crawl Spaces under Buildings

Garbage bags, tin cans or other open containers may collect water. Refuse may attract vermin whose droppings will make the area even more enticing to *Culex*. Trash or garbage of any kind should be removed .

Containment Areas for Livestock

Pens should be examined for permanent or semi-permanent puddles, or low, outlying areas of standing water that receive runoff. Steps should be taken to reduce the amount of runoff and fill in the puddles. Disposal of animal wastes should be done in an area with drainage sufficient to prevent the accumulation of rainwater.

Garbage Dumps

Areas should be examined for the presence of standing fresh water (in cans or can covers, trash bags, old buckets, under or beside storage sheds). Containers should be overturned or adequately covered and puddles filled in.

Gas Tanks

Area should be examined for the presence of refuse, standing fresh water or containers able to collect standing water. Refuse should be removed, puddles filled, and containers covered or overturned.

Clogged Ditches or Drains

Remove source of clog and check routinely.

Garbage Cans, Recycle Bins and Other Containers

Holes should be punched in the bottoms (not the sides) of plastic garbage or recycling bins to prevent them from holding water. All areas with significant human impact should be examined for forgotten or discarded containers (flower pots, tin cans, buckets, etc.) that may fill with fresh water and provide breeding habitat. Containers should be discarded, covered or overturned.

Tire ruts on roads

Tire ruts can prove to be significant breeding ground for freshwater mosquitoes. The ruts should be filled and the road graded to improve drainage.

Note: If potential breeding sites are found that are not easy to remedy by the means outlined above, the location and a brief description of the area should be given to the park biologist in charge of mosquito management.

APPENDIX 3

2003 Annual Report of the Fire Island National Seashore (FIIS) Mosquito Surveillance and Management Program

Stacey Kopitsch
Fire Island National Seashore, Patchogue, NY 11772

ABSTRACT

The Fire Island National Seashore (FIIS) mosquito surveillance and management program was implemented in 1998 in response to public concern over Eastern Equine Encephalitis (EEE), and later West Nile Virus (WNV). Since 2000, WNV has been detected within the park every year. In 2000 it was detected in the community of Saltaire, in 2001 it was detected at Watch Hill, and in 2002 it was detected again at Watch Hill (near the border of the Davis Park community) and in the Wilderness Area.

The 2003 mosquito trapping season began the week of June 2, 2003 and was terminated the week of October 13, 2003. A total of 12 mosquito traps were maintained at 5 different study sites within the park. The 5 study sites chosen were the Fire Island Lighthouse Tract, Sailors Haven, Watch Hill, the Wilderness Area and the William Floyd Estate. Mosquito numbers were generally low at the start and end of the trapping season and peaked in late June and July. Light traps typically yielded greater numbers of mosquitoes than gravid traps by orders of magnitude. The highest light trap total was an estimated 21,000 mosquitoes obtained from a light trap located in the Wilderness Area. Compared with past years, the numbers of *Culex spp.* caught in light traps this year was fairly low. A possible explanation for these lower than usual numbers may be that the start of the 2003 season was extremely wet, which may have actually inhibited breeding. For 2003, the highest gravid trap total was 154 mosquitoes, 137 of which were *Culex spp.* These were obtained from a gravid trap located at the William Floyd Estate. The larval sampling that was done produced insignificant numbers (> 10 larvae per dip).

WNV was isolated from 3 pools of *Culex spp.* caught at the William Floyd Estate. One pool was collected on 8/18/03 and two pools were collected on 8/26/03. The park's first WNV positive bird was also collected this year in the community of Cherry Grove on 8/12/03. Interestingly, a new mosquito-borne virus was found in the park this year at Watch Hill, with a pool of *O. sollicitans* collected on 9/4/03 that tested positive for Cache Valley Virus.
Key words: Cache Valley Virus, Culex spp., Eastern Equine Encephalitis, gravid trap, light trap, Aedes sollicitans, West Nile Virus.

INTRODUCTION

Fire Island is a 32-mile long barrier island situated off the south shore of Long Island, New York. A unit of the National Park Service, Fire Island National Seashore (FIIS) comprises 26 miles of this narrow barrier island and is characterized by salt marsh, dune grassland, dune shrubland, interdunal swale and forest/shrubland habitat (Klopfer et al. 2002). Created in 1964, FIIS is maintained and operated by the National Park Service, under Department of the Interior regulation and jurisdiction. Within the boundaries of the park lie the historic William Floyd Estate, the Otis G. Pike Wilderness area, park-maintained lands such as Sailors Haven and Watch Hill, as well as 17 private resort communities. All of FIIS falls within the boundaries of Suffolk County, Long Island. At the West end, FIIS is bounded by the Robert Moses State Park and on the East end by the Smith Point County Park (figure 1).

In 1998 FIIS implemented a mosquito surveillance and management program in response to concerns that Eastern Equine Encephalitis (EEE), a mosquito-borne virus, could potentially occur within the park. This new program also served as a model study for other national parks to follow. When another mosquito-borne virus, West Nile Virus (WNV), was found in the New

50

York region in 1999, mosquito surveillance and management efforts were subsequently increased within the park. Every year since, WNV has been detected at various locations within FIIS. In 2000, WNV was detected in the community of Saltaire. In 2001, it was detected at Watch Hill. In 2002 it was detected in both Watch Hill (near the border of the Davis Park community) and in the Wilderness Area.

Approximately 40 mosquito species have been recorded from Suffolk County, Long Island (Guirgis 1984). Approximately 25 of these species have been recorded throughout FIIS (table 1) (Lussier 2003). Of these species, the FIIS mosquito surveillance and management program focuses on *Culex pipiens*, *Culex restuans*, *Culex salinarius*, and *Aedes sollicitans*. All four of these species are potential vectors for WNV, and *Aedes sollicitans* is also a potential vector for EEE. The preferred habitats for *Culex pipiens* are areas that contain standing water with high organic content. This could be natural areas such as roadside ditches or artificial containers such as barrels, discarded tires and wells, or heavily polluted water such as in sewage treatment plants (Means 1987). The breeding of *Culex pipiens* is continuous throughout the summer months and peaks in August (Means 1987). Like *Culex pipiens*, *Culex restuans* also prefer breeding habitats that are rich in organic content. *Culex restuans* are often misidentified as *Culex pipiens* and vice versa, as their appearance is almost identical, except for the scales that are present on their mesothorax (Means 1987). *Culex salinarius* breeds in a wide range of habitats, but is exceptionally abundant in freshwater marshes in Suffolk County (Means 1987). *Aedes sollicitans*, formerly classified as *Aedes sollicitans* and also known as the white-banded salt marsh mosquito, is abundant in the salt marshes of Suffolk County (Means 1979). Adults emerge by mid-May and can produce successful generations into late September and even October (Means 1979).

The FIIS mosquito program relies on two important documents, the Mosquito Surveillance and Management Protocol and the Mosquito Action Plan (MAP). These are updated annually in collaboration with county, state and federal organizations, including Suffolk County Vector Control (SCVC) and Suffolk County Department of Health Services. These documents contain specific criteria for varying levels of alert and action, as well as the procedures for handling dead birds, the management of freshwater sources and equipment requirements.

METHODS

Study Sites

A total of five locations to be used as study sites were selected in consultation with Dr. Howard Ginsberg of the USGS. The selection of sites was based on vegetative indicators and either the presence of standing water or indications of water table surfacing. The five study sites established were 1) the Lighthouse Tract, 2) Sailor's Haven, 3) Watch Hill, 4) the Wilderness Area, 5) the William Floyd Estate.

The Fire Island Lighthouse is on the western border of FIIS, adjacent to Robert Moses State Park. The Lighthouse Tract is characterized by northern dune shrubland, maritime deciduous scrub forest, brackish meadow, highbush blueberry shrub forest and northern beach grass dune vegetation (Klopfer et al. 2002). Kismet Pond is also located here, which is a permanent, freshwater inland pool.

Sailors Haven is a park-maintained area of Fire Island that consists of a public marina, a visitor center and hiking trails. The Sunken Forest is the dominant feature of Sailors Haven, consisting of maritime holly forest, maritime decidious scrub forest and coastal oak-heath forest (Klopfer et al. 2002). Sailors Haven is adjacent to the community of Cherry Grove.

Like Sailors Haven, Watch Hill is a park-maintained area consisting of a public marina, visitor center and hiking trails. Watch Hill is characterized by northern dune shrubland, northern beach grass dune, pitch pine dune woodland, pitch pine oak forest, maritime deciduous scrub forest, highbush blueberry shrub forest, reedgrass marsh and northern salt shrub vegetation (Klopfer et al. 2002). Watch Hill is adjacent to the community of Davis Park.

The Otis G. Pike Wilderness Area is the only federally designated Wilderness Area in New York State and the entire Northeast. It is characterized by low and high saltmarsh, northern dune shrubland, northern salt shrub, reedgrass marsh, brackish meadow habitat, highbush blueberry shrub forest, brackish interdunal swale and beach heather dune vegetation (Klopfer et al. 2002). The Wilderness Area is bordered on the east by Smith Point County Park.

Though not located on the barrier island, the historic William Floyd Estate became a part of FIIS in 1976. The estate consists of 640 acres located in Mastic, NY on Long Island. It is dominated by coastal oak-heath forest and also characterized by cultivated pasture, pitch pine-oak forest, reedgrass marsh, high salt marsh, maritime deciduous scrub forest, acidic red maple basin swamp forest and northern salt shrub vegetation (Klopfer et al. 2002).

Equipment

Two types of traps were used for the collection of mosquitoes: CDC Gravid traps (John W. Hock Company model #1712) and CDC Miniature Light traps (John W. Hock Company model #512). The gravid traps were designed to attract and collect gravid (egg-bearing) *Culex* mosquitoes. Gravid mosquitoes were the preferred specimens for testing WNV as they have already fed and are therefore more likely to be infected with the virus than those mosquitoes which have not yet fed. The gravid traps consisted of PVC tubing that had a basic motor and fan secured inside. These were powered by a sealed 6-volt battery. The PVC tubing rested on top of a bin that contained an organic, fermented mixture of grass, rabbit feed and water. The traps were adjusted so that the base of each tube sat approximately 1 inch above the surface of the mixture. As gravid mosquitoes approached the organic mixture to lay their eggs, the fan pulled the mosquitoes up into the tubing and into a net placed at the top of the tubing (figure 2).

The light traps were designed to attract and collect host-seeking adult female mosquitoes of all species. As with the gravid traps, the light traps consisted of a basic motor and fan secured inside a tube and powered by a battery. In order to attract mosquitoes to the light trap, a block of 6" x 6" x 6" dry ice was wrapped in newspaper and hung adjacent to the trap. Carbon dioxide gas given off during sublimation of the dry ice attracted mosquitoes to the vicinity of the trap. Once baited, an incandescent light located at the top of the trap drew the mosquitoes to the trap, upon which the fan pulled them down inside the tubing and into a collection container at the bottom (figure 3).

Personal protection equipment was a necessity for the field work done for the mosquito program. A white, disposable Tyvek™ suit with a hood and elastic wrists and ankles was worn for protection against ticks and mosquito bites. A hoop-ring headnet and leather gloves were also worn for protection against mosquito bites. Rubber hip waders were worn for when hiking in wet areas and also provided a smooth surface that inhibited ticks from grasping on.

Trapping Schedule

The mosquito trapping season began the week of June 2, 2003 and ended the week of October 13, 2003. The season began with a total of 10 traps established at the five study sites. Two additional traps were established later in the season to give a total of 12 traps that were maintained within FIIS. Traps were typically set in the afternoon, left overnight and then picked up the following morning. Care was taken not to leave the traps out for longer than 12 hours, as the specimens could dry out. Ideally, each trap was to be set once per week. Dry ice for the light traps was purchased from Brookhaven National Laboratory (BNL). Ice pickups were scheduled for every Tuesday morning at BNL. At the start of the season, the mosquito technician took a 4 hour safety at BNL to obtain a pass to enter the Brookhaven campus.

Multiple traps were maintained at each study site, however the Lighthouse Tract location was an exception in that only a single gravid trap was maintained there. This trap was positioned opposite Kismet pond (figure 4).

At the start of the 2003 season, the Sailor's Haven location contained 2 traps, a gravid trap located within the Sunken Forest and a light trap positioned behind the concessions building. After a dead crow from Cherry Grove tested positive for WNV, a second light trap was added on 8/28/03 near the Cherry Grove border, bringing the total to 3 traps at the Sailors Haven location (figure 5).

A total of 3 traps were positioned at Watch Hill: 2 gravid traps and 1 light trap. The light trap and one of the gravid traps were situated near the border of the Davis Park community near a temporary woodland pool. These two traps were referred to as Watch Hill West gravid trap and Watch Hill Light trap. Two traps were placed at this location because WNV had been detected there the previous year. The other gravid trap was located next to house #12 in a reedgrass marsh near the fire break. This trap was referred to as Watch Hill gravid trap (figure 6).

The Wilderness Area contained 1 light trap and 1 gravid trap. The light trap was positioned between the low and high marsh on the bay side, approximately 1 kilometer west of the Wilderness Visitor Center at Smith Point. This location was referred to as Smith Shores. The gravid trap was positioned approximately ¾ of a kilometer east of Old Inlet, directly on Burma Road. This location was referred to Hospital Point (figure 7).

The William Floyd Estate initially had 2 gravid traps. One was located near the salt marsh at the eastern border of the estate, and was thus referred to as the William Floyd Estate East gravid trap. The other trap was located in the forest on the western border and thus referred to as the William Floyd Estate West gravid trap. A light trap was added at the western location on 7/28/03, following a false positive WNV test result (and three subsequent positives) at this location. This trap was referred to as the William Floyd Estate light trap (figure 8). For all trap locations, Universal Transverse Mercator (UTM) coordinates were generated using a Garmin[TM] Global Positioning System (GPS) unit.

In anticipation of high winds associated with a nearby Hurricane, all trap equipment was removed from the island and the William Floyd Estate on 9/16/03 and 9/17/03. Following the passage of the storm, the 2 gravid traps at the William Floyd Estate were re-established for one additional week and then removed. All of the light traps were re-established and set through the week of October 13, 2003, when the trapping season was terminated.

Transportation

Compared to other developed barrier islands, Fire Island is unique in that it does not have a paved road, therefore not all traps could be reached by vehicle. Of the five study sites, only the Lighthouse, the William Floyd Estate and the Smith Shores light trap could be reached by vehicle. The traps located at Sailors Haven, Watch Hill and Hospital Point could only be reached by boat. This method of transportation was highly weather-dependent and so the trapping schedule varied each week according to the forecast. During inclement weather, traps that needed to be set by boat sometimes could not be set and so incomplete data was obtained for the week. Ferries that operated to both Sailors Haven and Watch Hill were sometimes used during inclement weather. Two vessels were used for monitoring at the locations only accessible by boat. These were 21' and 17' open vessels with single outboard engines. A van was used for those traps accessible by vehicle. Though never done, it was also possible to use a 4-wheel drive vehicle to drive along the beach. This would only have been permitted after Labor Day when the FIIS beach driving season was reopened.

Adult Mosquito Sampling and Analysis

After being established at a particular location, most of the trap equipment remained at that trap site until the end of the season. The only equipment that was removed and reset each week were the batteries, the collection nets and any remaining dry ice. Immediately after being picked up in the mornings, the collection nets were placed in a cooler with dry ice to preserve the specimens and knock them unconscious so that they could later be analyzed. If the specimens were wet upon being picked up, the collection nets were hung indoors and allowed to dry thoroughly before placing them on dry ice.

The analysis of mosquitoes involved determining the total number of mosquitoes caught per trap, the total numbers of *Culex spp.* and *O. sollicitans* caught per trap, and the isolation of mosquito pools to be sent for arbovirus testing. For traps that contained relatively few mosquitoes (less than 500), all individual mosquitoes were counted to determine the total number caught, the total number of *Culex spp.* caught and the total number of *O. sollicitans* caught. For traps that contained high numbers of mosquitoes (greater than 500), the total number of mosquitoes in that trap was estimated using sample size: mass ratios. The contents of the entire trap were weighed using a triple beam balance, and the resulting mass compared to the mass of a known sub-sample size (between 100 and 300 mosquitoes) from that same trap. The following formula was used:

$$T = (\text{\# of mosquitoes in sub-sample})(\text{mass of all mosquitoes}) \div \text{mass of sub-sample}$$

where T = the total number of mosquitoes in a single trap.

For traps with high numbers of mosquitoes, the total number of *Culex spp.* and *O. sollicitans* were also estimated. This was done by determining the percentage of *Culex spp.* or

*O. sollicitan*s in that known sub-sample, and then multiplying that percentage by the estimated total number of mosquitoes. To estimate the total number of *Culex spp.* in a single trap the following formula was used:

$$\% \text{ of Culex} = (\text{\# of Culex in sub-sample} \div \text{total \# of individuals in sub-sample}) \text{ x } 100$$

$$T_C = \% \text{ of Culex } x \text{ } T$$

where T_C = the total number of *Culex spp.* in a single trap. To estimate the total number of *O. sollicitans* in a single trap the same formula was used:

$$\% \text{ of } O. \text{ sol.} = (\text{\# of } O. \text{ sol. in sub-sample} \div \text{total \# of individuals in sub-sample}) \text{ x } 100$$

$$T_{sol} = \% \text{ of } O. \text{ sollicitans } x \text{ } T$$

where T_{sol} = the total number of *O. sollicitans* in a single trap.

After estimating the total number of *Culex spp.* and *O. sollicitans*, the species in each trap were sorted. Individual *Culex spp.* and *O. sollicitans* were pulled out to form pools. A pool consisted of 10 to 50 mosquitoes of the same species collected from the same trap at the same time. Depending on the time constraints each day, as many pools as possible of *Culex spp.* were picked out. More emphasis was put on picking out pools of *Culex spp.*, as WNV was a more immediate threat on FIIS than EEE. Therefore a maximum of only 3 *O. sollicitans* pools were usually picked out of each trap. Pools were placed in petri dishes, secured with rubber bands and labeled with the type of trap (gravid or light), the trap location, the date set and the contents of the pool (# of mosquitoes and species). Pools were then stored on dry ice until they could be transported to Suffolk County Vector Control. Once at SCVC, they were stored in a dry ice freezer until being sent to the New York State Department of Health Wadsworth Center in Albany for arbovirus testing. Results of the laboratory testing took approximately 2 weeks to get back.

Larval Sampling and Analysis

As time permitted, larval sampling was done in areas that have had positive WNV pools, either from 2003 (William Floyd Estate), or in previous years (Wilderness Area and Watch Hill). Sampling was done along transects, preferably in an East to West direction. A standard pint-dipper with an extended handle was used for sampling (Service 1976). For salt marsh sampling, transects were walked for 80 steps, with one dip taken per step, on alternate sides giving a total of 80 dips. Freshwater transects followed the same procedure except that they were walked for only 25 steps giving a total of 25 dips. Whether or not the dipper encountered wet or dry ground was recorded, as well as the number of mosquito larvae in each dip. A representative sample of larvae from the entire transect was saved in a Nalgene^{TM} container and labeled with the date, time and location collected. Once back at the lab, larvae were analyzed under a stereoscopic microscopic and a key was used to determine species. Individual species were then transferred into glass vials containing ethanol to be stored.

RESULTS

Light Traps

For 2003, the total numbers of mosquitoes caught in light traps exhibited a bimodal curve. The traps yielded low numbers at the start of the season followed by an increase during the end of June and July. There was then a decrease during the months of August and September, followed by a slight increase again during late September into October (figure 9). The highest total came from the Smith Shores trap on 6/30/03, with an estimated 21,000 mosquitoes. The Smith Shores light trap averaged 5800 mosquitoes, the Watch Hill light trap averaged 2200 mosquitoes, the Sailors Haven light trap averaged 1700 mosquitoes, the Sailors Haven West light trap averaged 381 mosquitoes and the William Floyd Estate light trap averaged 273 mosquitoes during the 2003 season.

The total numbers of *Culex spp.* caught in the light traps also exhibited a bimodal curve (figure 10). The highest total of *Culex spp.* came from the Smith Shores trap on 6/30/03 with an estimated total of 6400. The Smith Shores light trap averaged 1900, the Watch Hill light trap averaged 1000, the Sailors Haven light trap averaged 55, the Sailors Haven West light trap averaged 238 and the William Floyd Estate light trap averaged 106 *Culex spp.* during the 2003 season.

The total numbers of *O. sollicitans* caught in the light traps exhibited a bell-shaped curve, with the lowest numbers occurring at the start and end of the season, and a peak occurring in the middle of the season (figure 11). The highest total of O. sollicitans came from the Smith Shores trap on 7/28/03 with an estimated total of 7200. The Smith Shores light trap averaged 1500, the Watch Hill light trap averaged 247, the Sailors Haven light trap averaged 14, the Sailors Haven West light trap averaged 5 and the William Floyd Estate light trap averaged 44 *O. sollicitans* during the 2003 season.

Gravid Traps

The total numbers of mosquitoes caught in gravid traps also exhibited a bell-shaped curve, with the lowest totals occurring at the start and end of the season, and the highest totals occurring in the middle of the season (Figure 12). The highest total came from the William Floyd Estate West gravid trap on 7/22/03, with a total of 154 mosquitoes. The William Floyd Estate West gravid trap averaged 47 mosquitoes and the William Floyd Estate East gravid trap averaged 10 mosquitoes during the season. The Hospital Point gravid trap averaged 27 mosquitoes, the Sunken Forest gravid trap averaged 11 mosquitoes and the Lighthouse gravid trap averaged 12 mosquitoes. The Watch Hill gravid trap averaged 14 mosquitoes and the Watch Hill West gravid trap averaged 16 mosquitoes during the 2003 season.

The total numbers of *Culex spp.* caught in gravid traps exhibited a bell-shaped curve as well (Figure 13). The highest total came from the William Floyd Estate West gravid trap on 7/22/03, with a total of 137 *Culex spp.* The William Floyd Estate West gravid trap averaged 40 and the William Floyd Estate East gravid trap averaged 7 *Culex spp.* during the season. The Hospital Point gravid trap averaged 14 and the Sunken Forest and Lighthouse gravid traps both averaged 9. The Watch Hill gravid trap averaged 7 and the Watch Hill West gravid trap averaged 14 gravid *Culex spp.* during the 2003 season.

The total numbers of *O. sollicitans* caught in gravid traps also exhibited a bell-shaped curve, however these numbers were much less than the number of *Culex spp.* caught (Figure 14). The highest total came from the Hospital Point gravid trap on 7/28/03, with a total of 49 *O. sollicitans*. Over the course of the season, the Hospital Point gravid trap averaged 10 *O. sollicitans*. The William Floyd Estate West gravid trap averaged 1 and the Lighthouse gravid trap averaged 2 *O. sollicitans*. The Watch Hill gravid trap averaged 3 and the Watch Hill West gravid trap averaged 2. No *O. sollicitans* were caught in both the William Floyd Estate East and the Sunken Forest gravid traps during the 2003 season.

Larvae

Five different larval species were identified from the larval sampling that was done (table 2). *Culex pipiens* were obtained from roadside ditches at the William Floyd Estate, *Culex salinarius* were obtained from the William Floyd marsh and *Anopheles spp.* were found in a small pond at the Estate. *Aedes vexans* and *Aedes canadensis* were both found in a temporary woodland pool at the Watch Hill West site. The five larval species that were found were not present in significant numbers (< 10 larvae per dip). No larvae were found when a transect was done at the Smith Shores marsh.

Arbovirus Testing

A dead crow collected from the Community of Cherry Grove on 8/12/03 tested positive for WNV. Virus was also isolated from three pools of *Culex spp.* from the William Floyd Estate West gravid trap. One of these pools was collected on 8/18/03 and the other two pools were collected on 8/26/03. On 10/6/03, the park was notified by SCVC that a pool of *O. sollicitans* collected on 9/4/03 from the Watch Hill light trap had a positive virus test result, possibly for EEE. This virus was later determined to be Cache Valley Virus.

DISCUSSION

Light Traps

The total number of mosquitoes and the total number of *Culex spp.* caught in light traps this year exhibited a bimodal curve. At the start of the season, these numbers were low, a possible explanation being the extremely wet start to the season (Figure 15). Approximately 12.27 inches of rain were recorded for the month of June, a month that typically averages 3.59 inches (Brookhaven National Laboratory 2003, Maghini 2003). The high amount of rain this season may have washed away eggs that were already laid and could have diluted already standing water, reducing the organic content and therefore making it not ideal for *Culex spp.* to breed. As the weather got warmer and drier, there was a peak in the total number of mosquitoes, and the total number of *Culex spp.* and *O. sollicitans* during late June and the month of July. Towards the middle of August and into September, there was then a decrease in the total number of mosquitoes, and of *Culex spp.* and *O. sollicitans*. Though temperatures were still fairly warm at this point, a possible explanation for this decline could be the desiccation of breeding habitat. Interestingly, in late September and into October, the total number of mosquitoes and *Culex spp.* caught in the light traps increased, despite the cooler weather. A possible explanation for this may be that there is breeding activity occurring in septic tanks in some of the communities (Davis Park). The exact species of *Culex* isolated from the light traps was not determined, however the identification of these species may offer more insight.

Gravid Traps

The total number of *Culex spp.* caught in the gravid traps exhibited a bell-shaped curve. The low numbers at the start of the season may also be explained by the wet weather. These numbers peaked in July and August, with the William Floyd Estate West gravid trap having the highest numbers. This is also the only location in the park from which WNV positive mosquitoes were isolated. By the first week in September, all of the gravid traps were catching numbers of *Culex spp.* that were insufficient to be sent for arbovirus testing (> 10 mosquitoes). Gravid trapping was therefore terminated the week of 9/22/03.

Other species of mosquitoes, including *O. sollicitans*, being caught in the gravid traps is incidental, as the gravid traps are designed for the collection of *Culex spp.* The discussion of these results therefore is irrelevant.

Larval Sampling

Larval sampling is done to monitor mosquito emergences and to located breeding habitat. If disease is present in an area of the park, larval sampling is critical for determining the possible need for control measures for the anticipated mosquito population. Due to time constraints, larval sampling at FIIS was very infrequent. When sampling was done is late July and August, potential breeding areas were often dry. Larvae that were collected were not found in significant numbers, as all sampling occasions produced fewer than 10 larvae per dip. The increase in *Culex spp.* numbers at the end of the season shows that these mosquitoes are still able to breed even during the cool weather. Attempts to locate *Culex spp.* breeding habitat however were unsuccessful, which again suggests that these mosquitoes are breeding in areas such as the septic tanks found in the communities of FIIS.

Arbovirus Testing

All positive test results were communicated to the mosquito biotechnician, park biologist and superintendent by Suffolk County Vector Control. Park staff were then notified of the results via email. Staff were advised to use personal protection and limit their exposure to areas with high mosquito densities. Interestingly, a new arbovirus was isolated at FIIS. Cache Valley virus (CV) was isolated from a pool of *O. sollicitans* collected on 9/4/03 from the Watch Hill

Light trap. The virus was first isolated in Utah in the 1950's and affects mainly livestock and is not thought to cause human disease, though there is a documented case of a deer hunter in North Carolina contracting Cache Valley virus (Sexton et al. 1997).

Important Issues

One very important issue that affects the FIIS mosquito program is the logistics associated with trapping. As Fire Island has no road, the logistics of trapping are very complicated. Setting each trap once per week could not always be done due to the problems associated with transportation on Fire Island. Trapping by boat was a necessity for several locations, however this method of transportation was not always reliable due to the weather. Often times, a trap could not be set due to inclement weather. Occasionally, the vessels used for trapping needed to be serviced, during which time the trapping schedule was further complicated. Using ferries as a method of transportation was sometimes a possibility, though could not be relied upon, especially prior to Memorial Day and after Labor Day as fewer trips were scheduled at these times. Driving on the beach was a possibility after Labor Day, though this too would have further complicated the trapping schedule, as the daily tides would need to be taken into account.

Another issue associated with the FIIS mosquito program is the failure and disturbance of equipment. Often times, a trap was disturbed or failed after being set, resulting in incomplete data. A particular problem this year occurred at the William Floyd Estate. For a period of several weeks, the west gravid trap was continuously overturned and its contents spilled. It was eventually determined from a footprint that a raccoon was knocking over this trap. The trap was relocated several meters away and never disturbed again.

Another issue that occurred this year was that following several positive pools in the Mastic Beach area of Long Island, Suffolk County Vector Control scheduled aerial pesticide spraying in the area. The William Floyd Estate is located within this area, and so would have been sprayed as well. After several correspondences between FIIS and SCVC, it was decided that aerial spraying would occur, but the William Floyd Estate would not be sprayed.

One final issue that affected the mosquito program this year was that of severe weather. In mid September, Hurricane Isabel had a projected storm path that included Long Island. The park went into incident command mode and all trap equipment was removed from the island and the William Floyd Estate. Following the passage of the storm, the light traps and the two William Floyd Estate gravid traps were reestablished. On 10/14/03 and 10/15/03 a high wind advisory was issued, with the forecasted winds being higher than what was experienced by Hurricane Isabel. The William Floyd Estate and Smith Shores light traps however were still set. Heavy flooding in the Wilderness Area prevented the Smith Shores trap from being picked up. When this trap was finally retrieved, both the trap and the battery suffered extensive damage from the wind and flooding.

Recommendations for the FIIS mosquito program

The position of mosquito biotechnician at FIIS is a seasonal one, and for this reason has a high amount of turnover. A new biotechnician must be trained almost on an annual basis, which is an overwhelming commitment. For example, being able to operate a motorboat is an essential skill for this program. The Motorboat Operator Certification Course (MOCC) offered by the park is a very challenging class. Even when taken early in the season, it takes weeks of dedicated practice in order to pass the MOCC boating exam. Until certified, the mosquito biotechnician requires a certified motorboat operator to accompany him/her when using a boat for either practice or trapping. The time commitment required for this significantly cuts into the commitments and duties of park motorboat operators. As a recommendation, motorboat skills should be a minimum qualification for the mosquito biotechnician prior to being hired.

To avoid a high turnover rate, the position of mosquito biotechnician could be made permanent. The biotechnician should primarily be responsible for the mosquito program, but as a permanent employee, could assist with other resource management programs after the trapping season. This would result in a more robust mosquito program and would also relieve some of the strain on resources experienced from the shortage of park staff.

Some of the equipment used for this program also needs to be upgraded. For example, when estimating the total number of mosquitoes in a trap, a triple beam balance with an accuracy of only 0.1g is used. These trap estimates therefore are extremely crude and inaccurate. The park should upgrade to an electronic balance with an accuracy of at least 0.001g for weighing such small masses as mosquitoes. Also, the majority of the traps used in the program are old, and several of them failed during the season. There was no adequate supply of replacement light traps this year and so new traps had to be ordered during the height of the season, a process which took several weeks. As a result, a light trap was not set at the William Floyd Estate for several weeks, and this was the location where WNV was isolated. For every trap established in the field, there should be a working, replacement trap kept on hand in the event that a trap should fail.

ACKNOWLEDGEMENTS

I wish to thank Marie Lawrence, as her time and dedication were essential for this program's functioning. I would like to thank Dr. Scott Campbell and Dr. Howard Ginsberg for their academic expertise. I also wish to thank Dawn Wiley and Heather Bosserman for their assistance with GPS data. Finally, I would like to thank members of the FIIS maintenance staff for their assistance with transportation.

LITERATURE CITED

Brookhaven National Laboratory. Monthly precipitation records. November 19, 2003
    <http:///www.bnl.gov/weather/4cast/precip.html>.

Guirgis, S. S. 1984. A new record of *Culiseta annulata* with notes on mosquito species in
    Suffolk County, Long Island, New York. Mosquito News **44**: 246.

Klopfer et al. 2002. NPS Vegetation Mapping Project at Fire Island National Seashore.
    Conservation Management Institute, Virginia Tech, Blacksburg, VA.

Lussier, C. 2003. Distribution and comparative trapping of mosquitoes in NPS units in
    the northeastern United States. Master's Thesis, University of Rhode Island,
    Kingston, RI.

Maghini, M. 2003. Wertheim National Wildlife Refuge weather station data. U. S. Fish
    and Wildlife Service, Shirley, NY.

Means, R. G. 1979. Mosquitoes of New York part I: the genus *Aedes* Meigen with
    identification keys to genera of Culicidae. The University of the State of New
    York, Albany, NY.

Means, R. G. 1987. Mosquitoes of New York part II: genera of Culicidae other
    than *Aedes* occurring in New York. The University of the State of New
    York, Albany, NY.

Service, M. W. 1976. Mosquito ecology: field sampling methods. Halsted Press, New
    York, NY.

Sexton. et al. 1997. Life-threatening Cache Valley virus infection. New England
    Journal of Medicine **336**: 547-549.

TABLES AND FIGURES FOR APPENDIX 3

Table 1. Mosquito species isolated from FIIS (Lussier 2003).

Species	Species
Aedes triseriatus	*Ochlerotatus canadensis*
Aedes vexans	*Ochlerotatus cantator*
	Ochlerotatus cinereus
Anopheles atropos	*Ochlerotatus excrusicans*
Anopheles punctipennis	*Ochlerotatus riparius*
Anopheles quadrimaculatis	*Ochlerotatus sollicitans*
	Ochlerotatus sticticus
Culex pipiens	*Ochlerotatus taeniorhynchus*
Culex restuans	*Ochlerotatus trivittatus*
Culex salinarius	
Culex territans	*Psorophora ciliata*
	Psorophora ferrox
Coquillettidia perturbans	
	Uranotaenis sappphirina
Culiseta impatiens	
Culiseta incidens	
Culiseta melanura	

Table 2. 2003 larval sampling results.

Date	Location	Habitat	Species	Number	Transect?
7/29/03	Smith Shores	marsh	N/A	0	yes
8/1/03	William Floyd Estate	marsh	*Culex salinarius*	15	yes
8/1/03	William Floyd Estate	roadside ditch	*Culex pipiens*	4	no
8/15/03	Watch Hill	woodland pool	*Ochlerotatus canadensis*	6	no
			Aedes vexans	1	
8/19/03	William Floyd Estate	pond	*Anopheles spp.*	4	yes

Figure 1. Map of Fire Island National Seashore

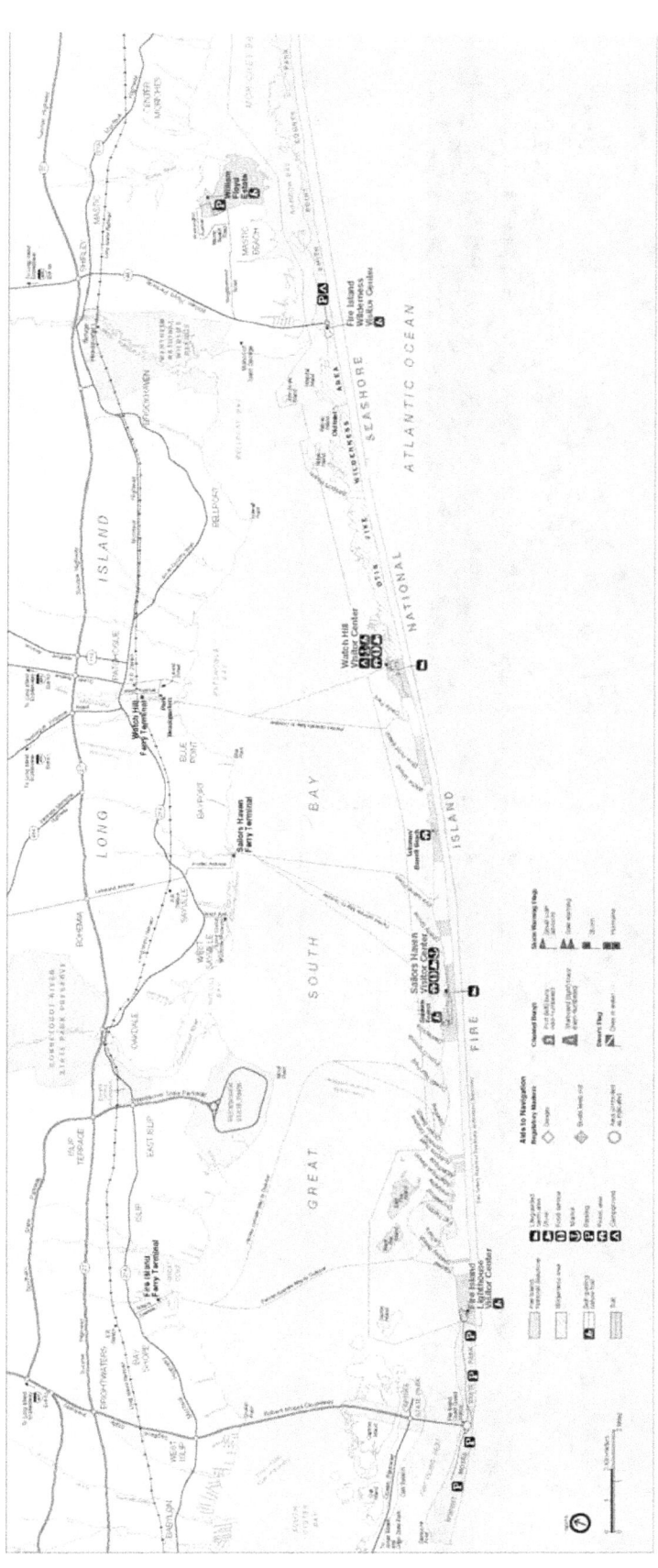

Figure 2. CDC Gravid trap with collection net and battery.

Figure 3. CDC Light trap with collection container.

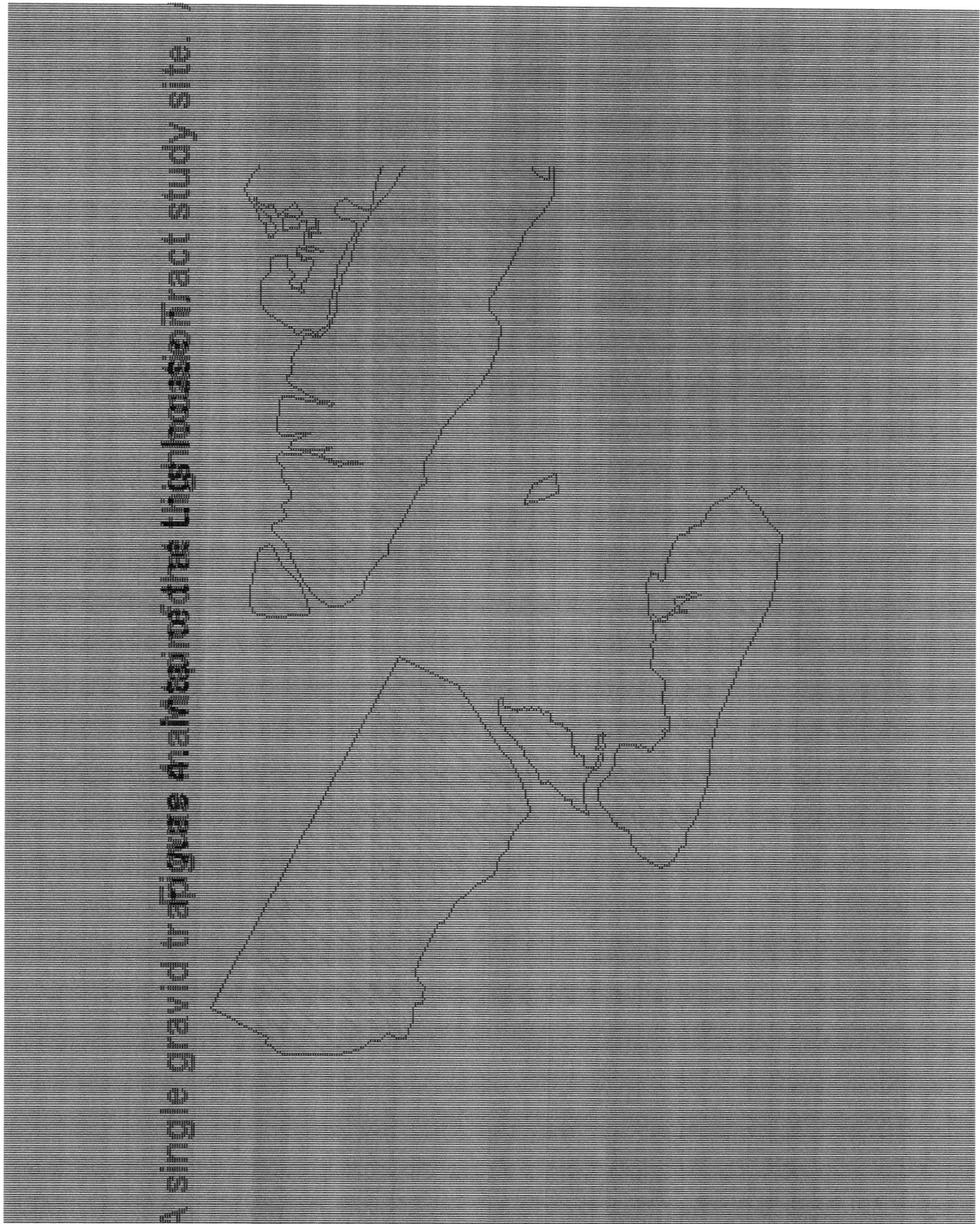

A single gravid triangulate Tursiops truncatus at study site.

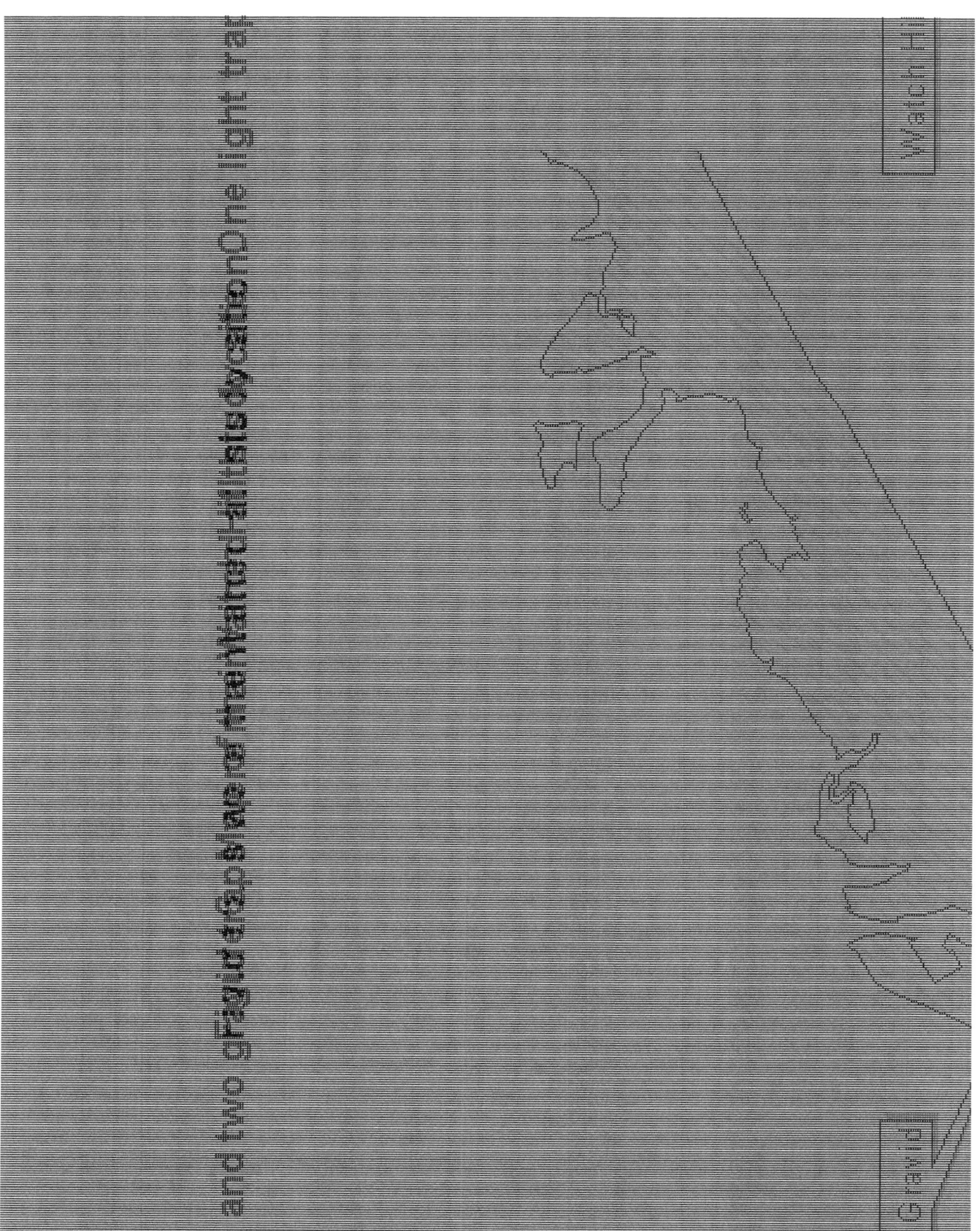

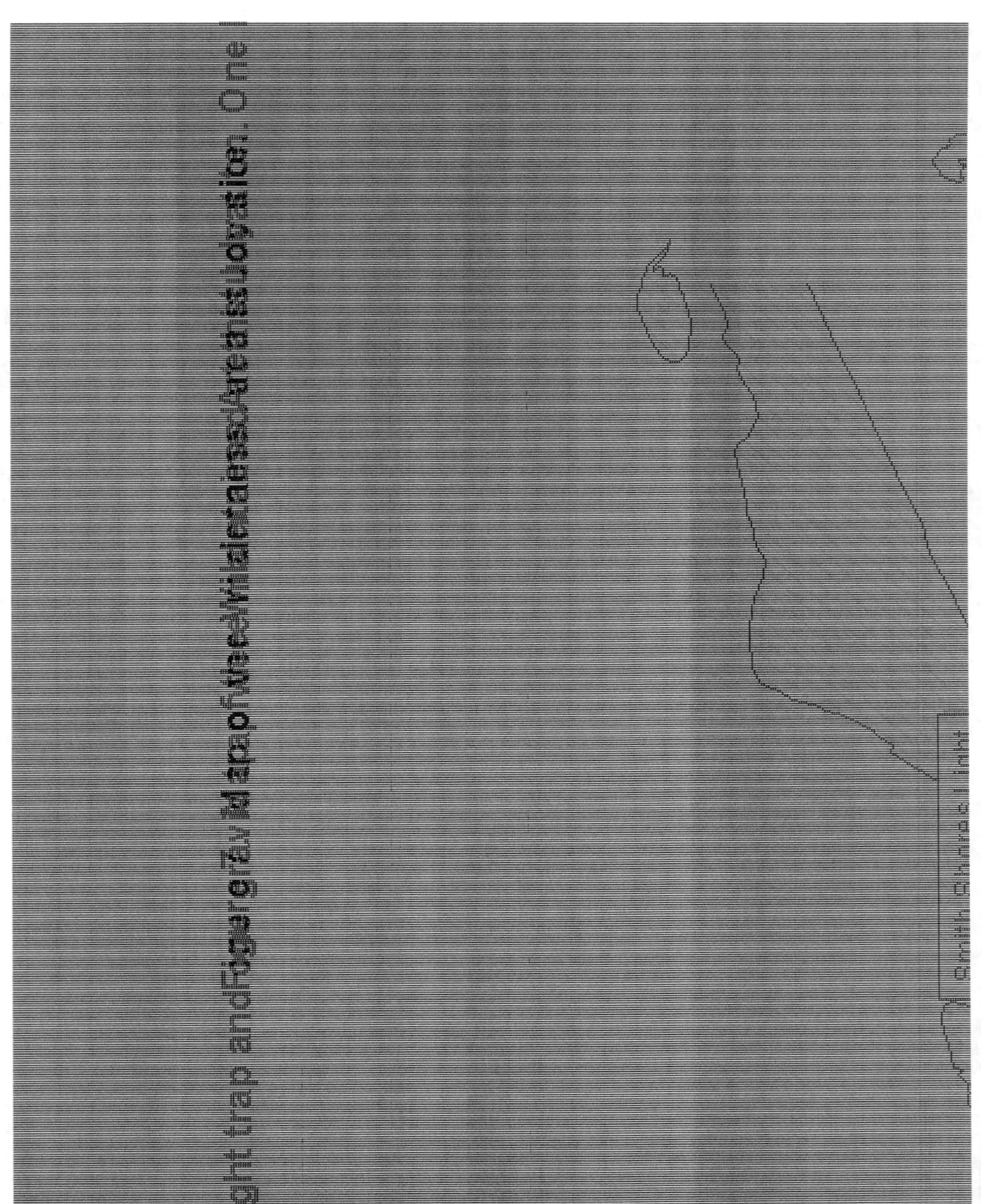

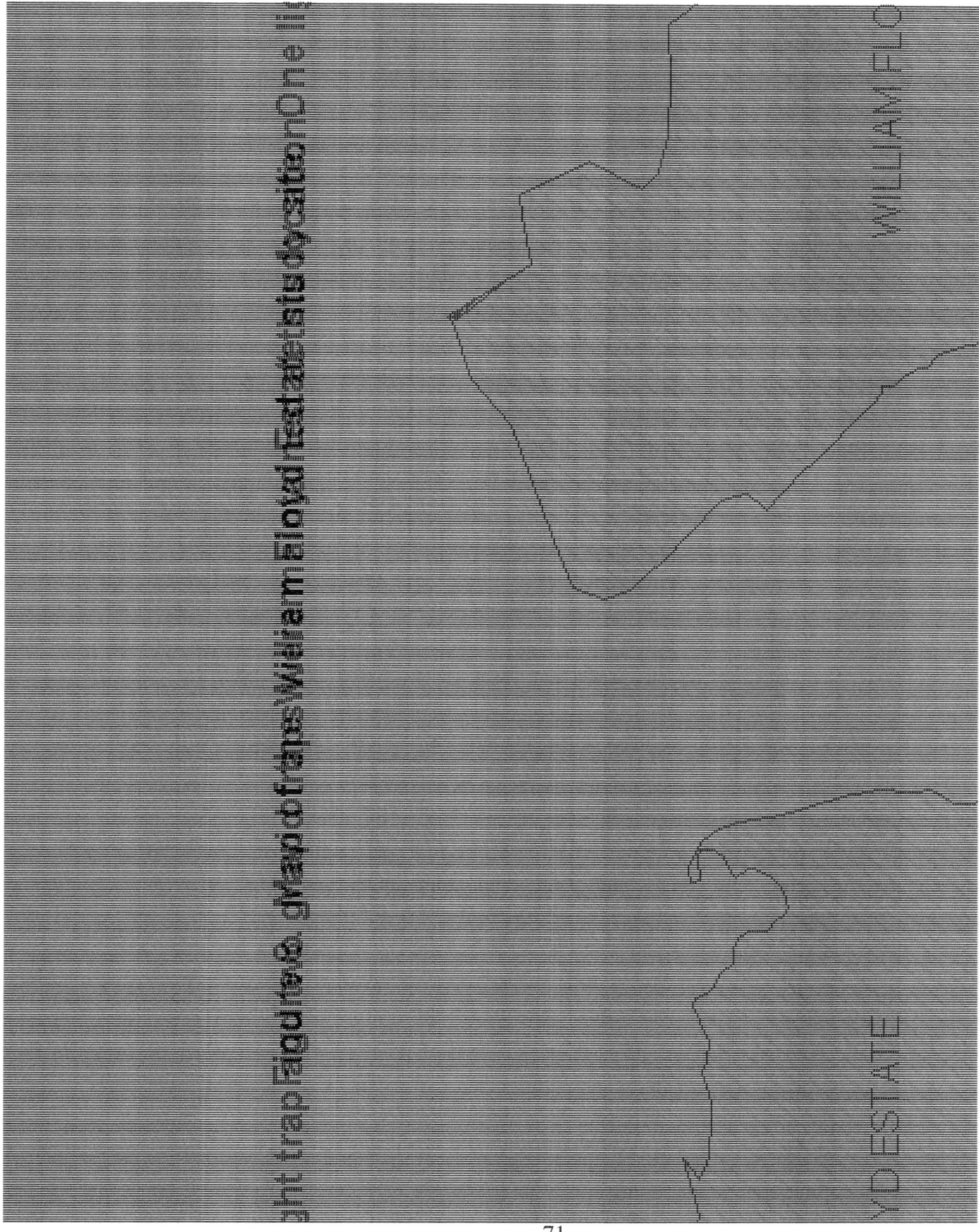

Figure 9. Total number of adult mosquitoes caught using light traps during the 2003 trapping season. Incomplete data indicates one of the following: No mosquitoes were caught, a trap was not set or a trap was disturbed/failed.

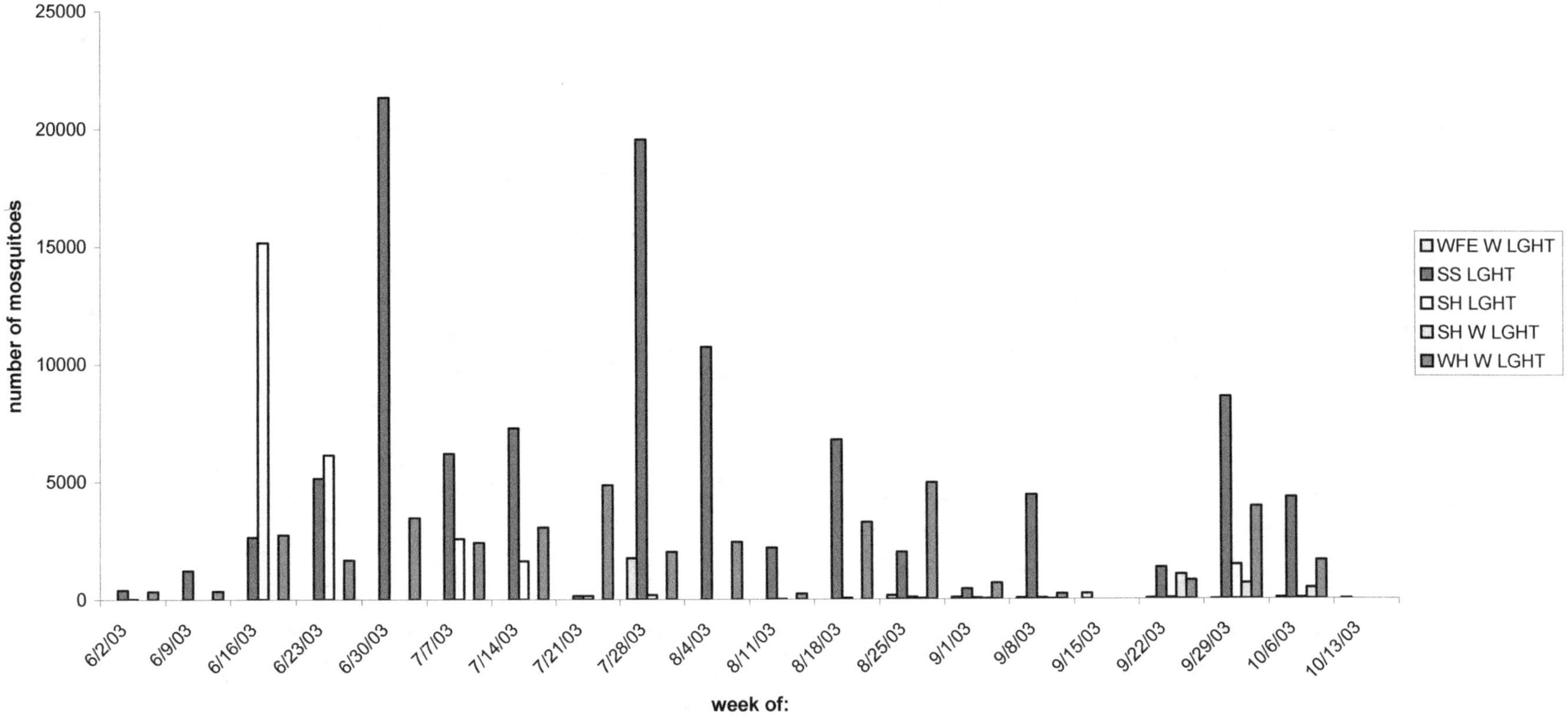

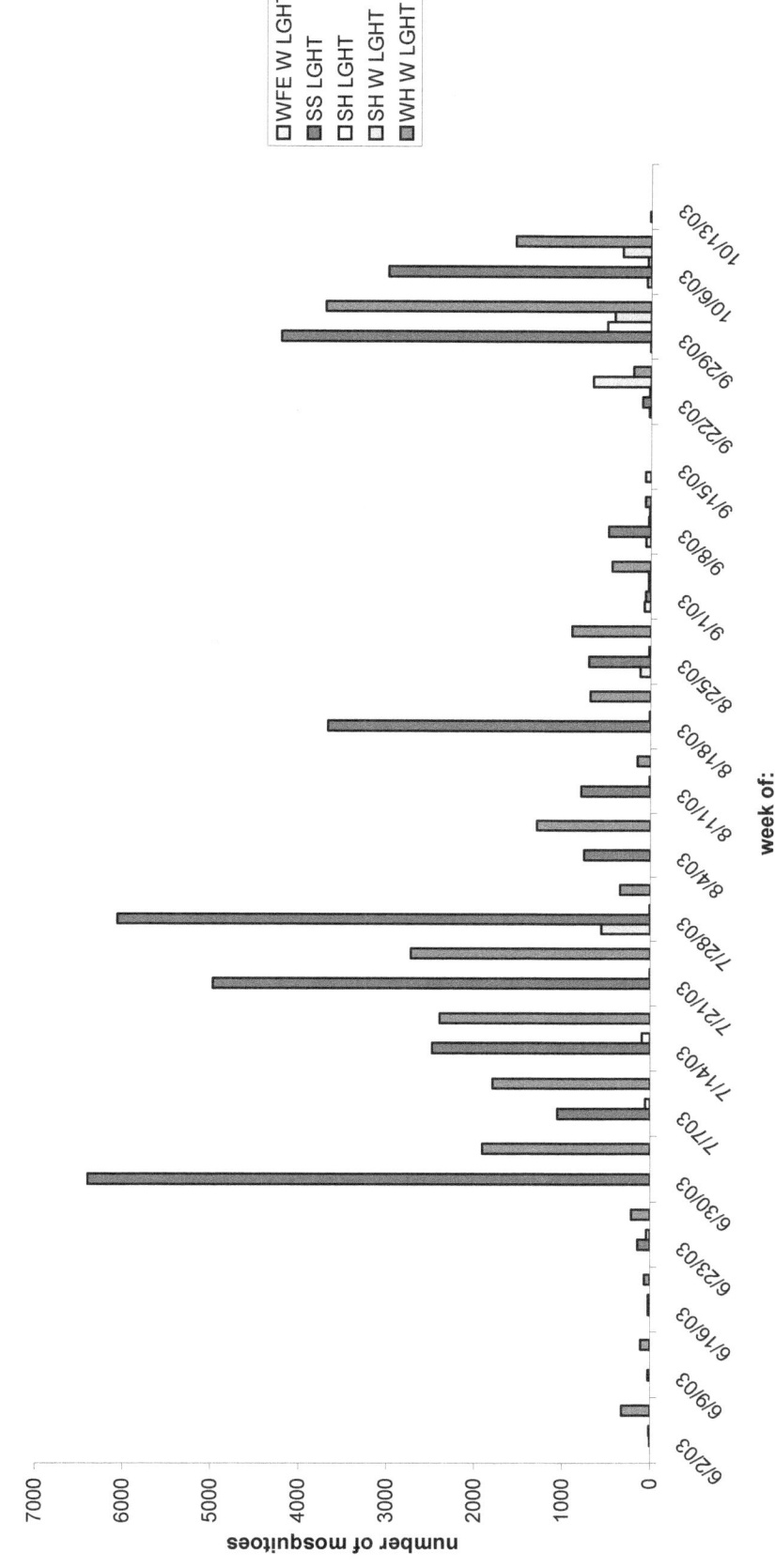

Figure 10. Total number of adult *Culex spp*. caught using light traps during the 2003 trapping season. Incomplete data indicates one of the following: no mosquitoes were caught, a trap was not set or a trap was disturbed/failed.

73

Figure 11. Total number of adult *O. sollicitans* caught using light traps during the 2003 trapping season. Incomplete data indicates one of the following: no mosquitoes were caught, a trap was not set or a trap was disturbed/failed.

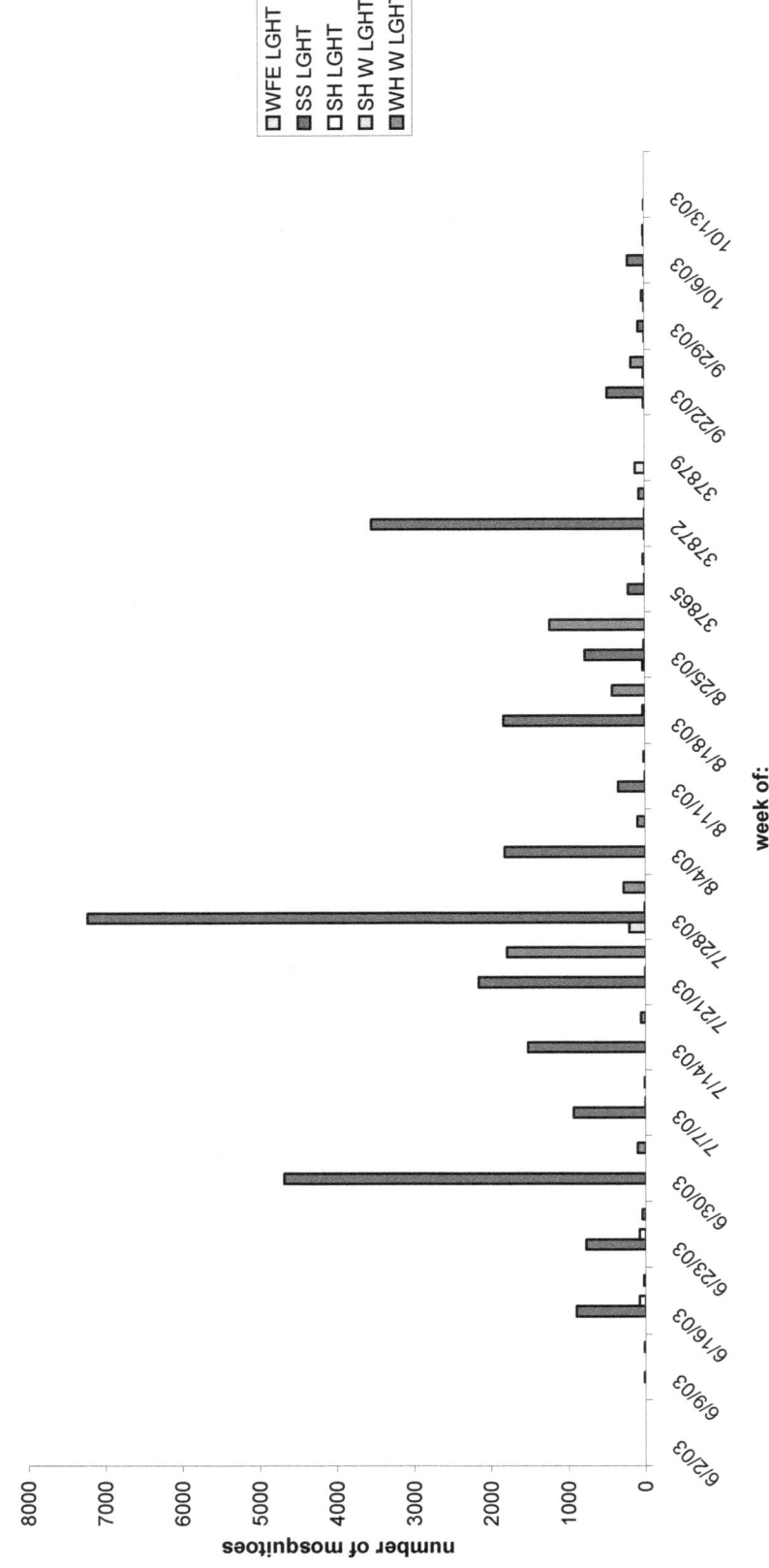

Figure 12. Total number of adult mosquitoes caught using gravid traps during the 2003 trapping season. Incomplete data indicates one of the following: no mosquitoes were caught, a trap was not set or a trap was disturbed/failed.

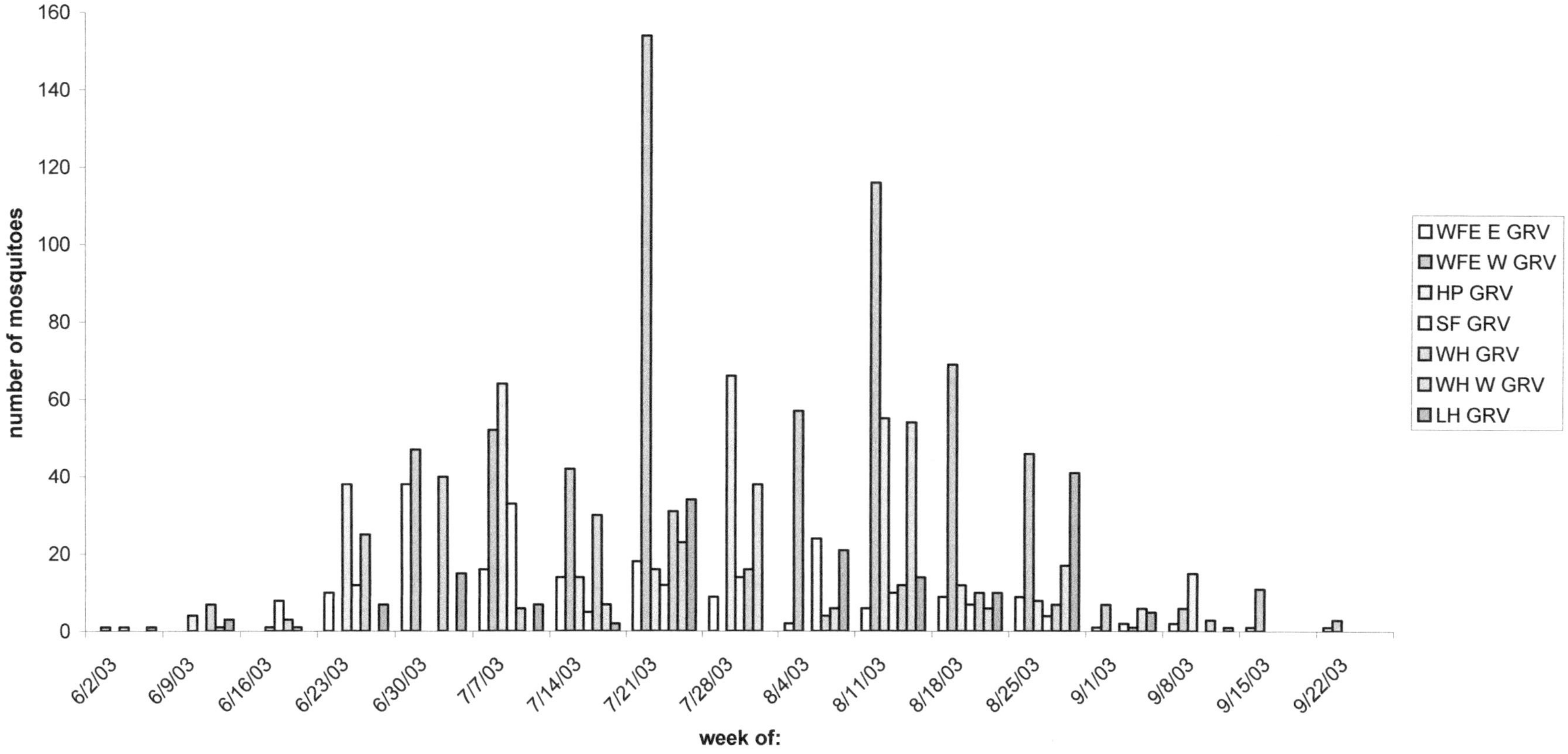

Legend:
- WFE E GRV
- WFE W GRV
- HP GRV
- SF GRV
- WH GRV
- WH W GRV
- LH GRV

week of:

number of mosquitoes

75

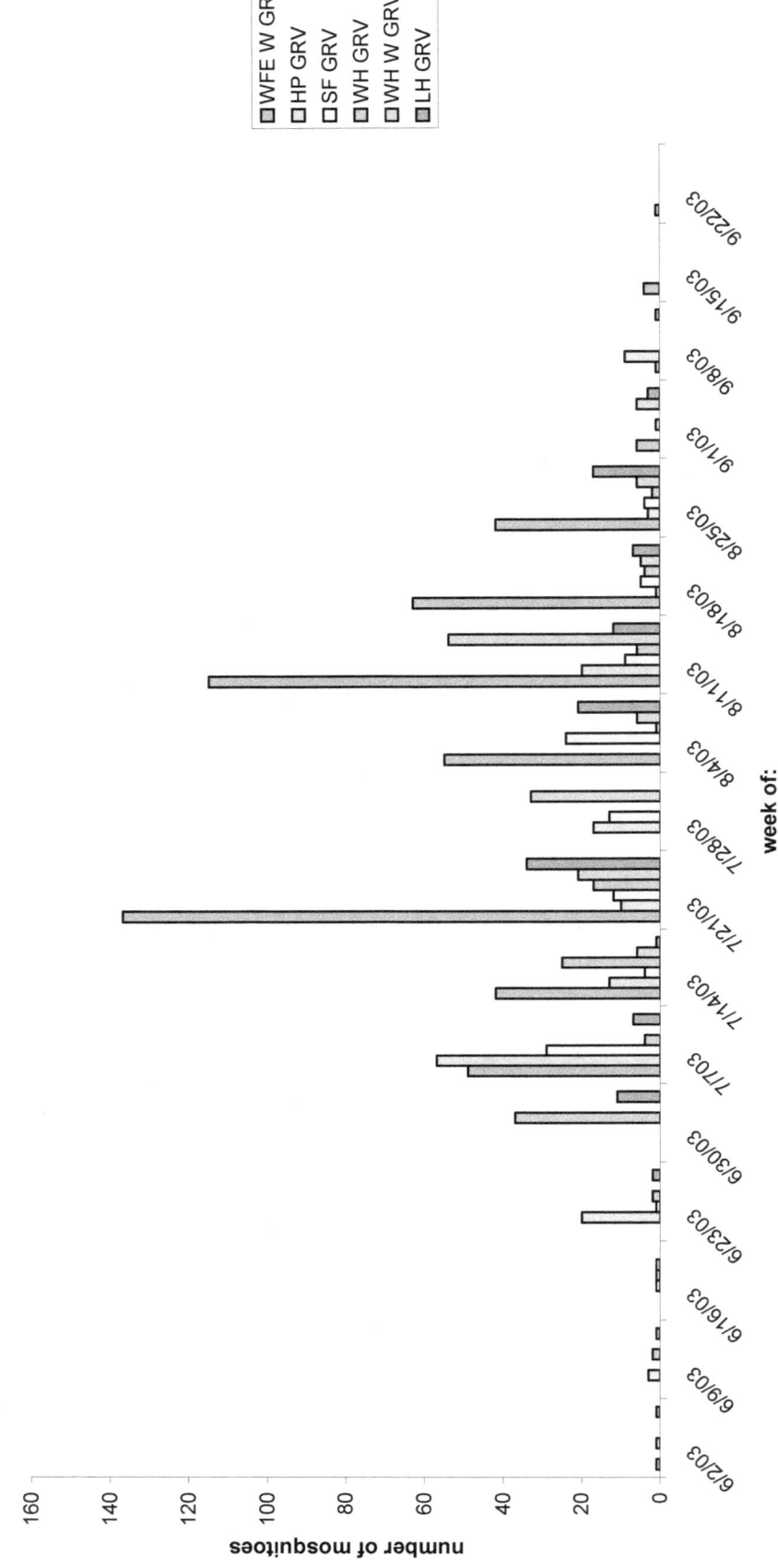

Figure 13. Total number of adult *Culex spp.* caught using gravid traps during the 2003 trapping season. Incomplete data indicates one of the following: no mosquitoes were caught, a trap was not set or a trap was disturbed/failed.

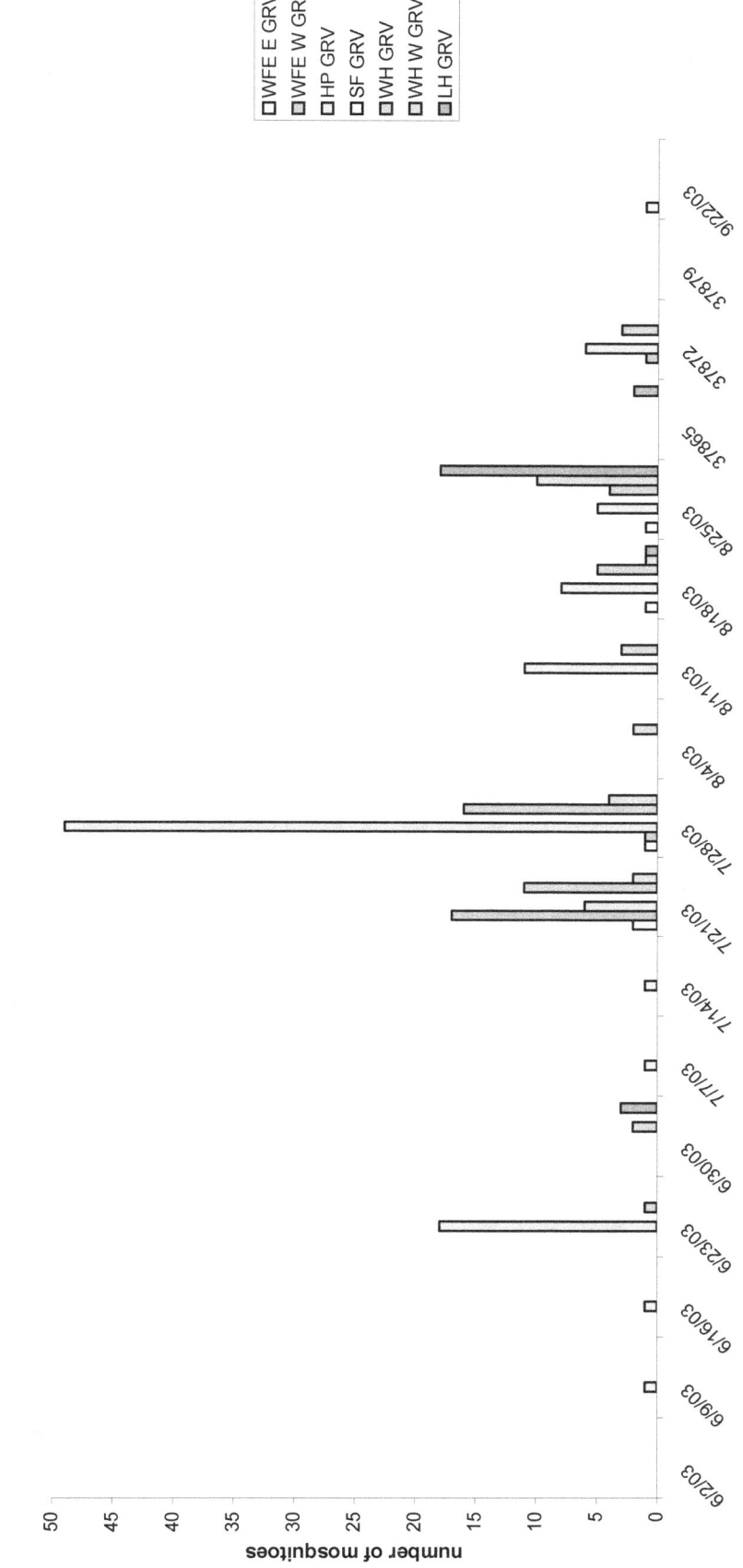

Figure 14. Total number of adult *O. sollicitans* caught using gravid traps during the 2003 trapping season. Incomplete data indicates one of the following: no mosquitoes were caught, a trap was not set or a trap was disturbed/failed.

77

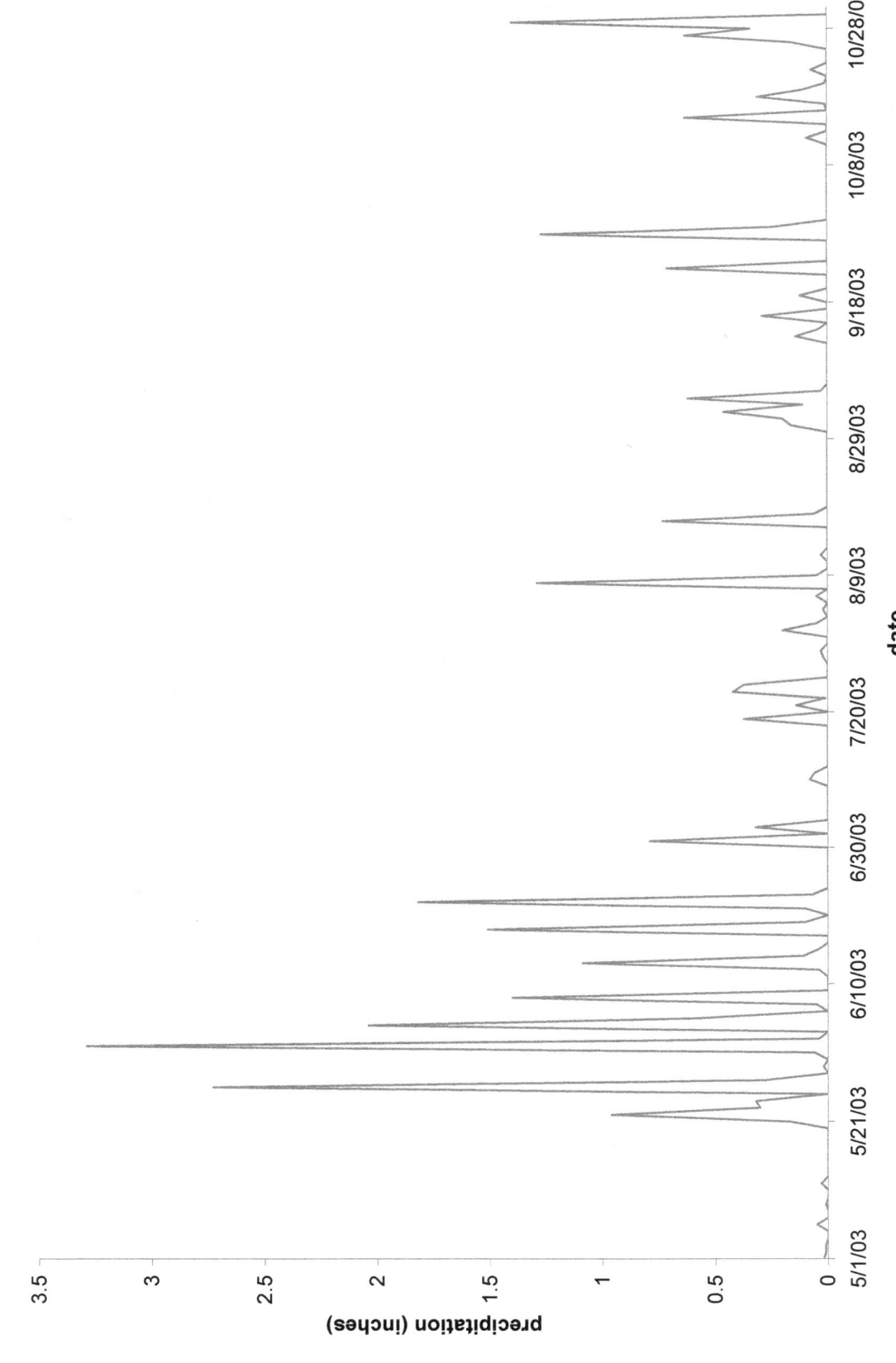

Figure 15. Daily precipitation during the 2003 mosquito trapping season. Data was obtained from the Wertheim National Wildlife Refuge weather station.

NPS D-110 September 2005

www.ingramcontent.com/pod-product-compliance
Lightning Source LLC
Chambersburg PA
CBHW081132290526
45795CB00006B/2210